CHARLOTTE BRONTË

Women Writers

General Editors: *Eva Figes* and *Adele King*

Published titles:

Forthcoming:

Further titles are in preparation

Women Writers

CHARLOTTE BRONTË

Pauline Nestor

BARNES & NOBLE BOOKS
TOTOWA, NEW JERSEY

© Pauline Nestor 1987

First published in the USA 1987 by
BARNES & NOBLE BOOKS
81 ADAMS DRIVE
TOTOWA, NEW JERSEY 07512

ISBN 0–389–20691–1
ISBN 0–389–20692–X (Pbk)

Printed in Hong Kong

Library of Congress Cataloging-in-Publication Data
Nestor, Pauline.
Charlotte Brontë.
(Women writers)
Bibliography: p.
Includes index.
1. Brontë, Charlotte, 1816–1855—Criticism and
interpretation. I. Title. II. Series.
PR4169.N47   1987   823′.8   86–22295
ISBN 0–389–20691–1
ISBN 0–389–20692–X (pbk.)

Contents

Acknowledgements

The task of writing this book has been made considerably
easier and more pleasurable by the congenial environment
created by my colleagues and students at Monash University.
I am grateful to my friends – especially Fay Lehmann, Rose
Lucas and the women of the Melbourne Feminist Critics
Group – for their interest and support. And once more my
particular thanks go to Marilyn Butler for her warm encouragement, valuable advice and generous practical assistance. Dr Butler's professionalism, enthusiasm and good
humour continue to offer example and inspiration.

Note on Texts

(*JE*) *Jane Eyre*, World Classics edn. (Oxford, Oxford
University Press, 1980).

(*P*) *The Professor* (London, Dent, 1980).

(*S*) *Shirley*, World Classics edn. (Oxford, Oxford University Press, 1981).

(*V*) *Villette* (Middlesex, Penguin, 1981).

(*LL*) *The Brontës: Their Lives, Friendships and Correspondence* eds T. J. Wise and J. A. Symington, 4 vols
(Oxford, Shakespeare Head, 1934).

Editors' Preface

The study of women's writing has been long neglected by a male critical establishment both in academic circles and beyond. As a result, many women writers have either been unfairly neglected, or have been marginalised in some way, so that their true influence and importance has been ignored. Other women writers have been accepted by male critics and academics, but on terms which seem, to many women readers of this generation, to be false or simplistic. In the past the internal conflicts involved in being a woman in a male-dominated society have been largely ignored by readers of both sexes, and this has affected our reading of women's work. The time has come for a serious reassessment of women's writing in the light of what we understand today.

This series is designed to help in that reassessment.

All the books are written by women, because we believe that men's understanding of feminist critique is only, at best, partial. And besides, men have held the floor quite long enough.

EVA FIGES
ADELE KING

1 Charlotte Brontë's Life

> . . . it is well that the true poet, quiet externally though he
> may be, has often a truculent spirit under his placidity, and
> is full of shrewdness in his meekness, and can measure the
> whole stature of those who look down on him, and
> correctly ascertain the weight and value of the pursuits
> they disdain him for not having followed. (*S* 49)

Charlotte Brontë lived most of her life as the dutiful daughter
of an Irish clergyman and died as the attentive wife of her
father's Irish curate. Yet even from her earliest years this
diminutive, short-sighted, desperately shy woman nourished
a feverish creativity and ambition, and in the ten short years
of her artistic maturity she created some of the century's most
potent heroines and rose to be acclaimed as the most
distinguished female author of her time, the writer who,
more than any other, 'impressed her mark so clearly on
contemporary literature' and drew 'so many followers to her
peculiar path'.[1] This apparent disjunction between the
modesty of Charlotte Brontë's life and person and the
magnitude of her literary achievement is symptomatic of a
life and character fraught with contradiction, division and
ambivalence.

The 'wild, strange facts' of the Brontë lives and the bleak
location of their life-long home on the rugged Yorkshire
moors have contributed a certain mystique to the Brontë
story. So, too, has the store of anecdotal evidence about the
eccentricities and idiosyncracies of the family – tales, for

example, of Emily's almost superhuman stoicism and detachment, Mr Brontë's erratic tyrannies and Branwell's dissoluteness. Perhaps overriding all is the desire to understand how such a concentration of genius occurred – how one family could nurture the diversity of talent reflected variously in *Jane Eyre*, *Wuthering Heights* and *The Tenant of Wildfell Hall*.

This fascination has its dangers, tempting critics to distort and trivialise Charlotte Brontë's life and its relevance to her work in two different ways. On the one hand, it can be romanticised as the exceptional life of an exceptional woman, seen as the stuff of legend and robbed of its day-to-day reality. On the other, the grinding difficulties and inequities of such a life can be stressed to the exclusion of all else, indulging another form of romanticisation by highlighting only Charlotte's repression and deprivation as a woman and an artist.

It is well to remember, then, that along with the apparent constrictions of her upbringing there were also liberating features. It is only with such a balanced view that we can begin to understand the deep divisions – between duty and rebellion, passion and repression, reason and feeling, reality and imagination – which so characterise both the woman and her work.

Charlotte Brontë was born on 21 April 1816 at Thornton in Yorkshire, the third child of six to Patrick and Maria Brontë. In her own terms, which reflect the nagging lack of physical self-esteem that dogged her throughout her life, Charlotte was the 'weakest, puniest, least promising of children'.[2]

In later life Charlotte regretted that she could remember very little of her mother, but the details of the early family history make that hardly surprising. Within seven years of her marriage Maria Brontë had borne six children and shortly after the family move to Haworth parsonage in April 1820, when the youngest child Anne was scarcely three months old,

Maria began to show symptoms of the illness from which she died in September of 1821.[3] With their mother growing steadily weaker and their father engrossed in the duties of a new parish, the children spent much time exploring the moors, establishing the habit of a lifetime which was to provide them with a deep sense of pleasure and freedom.

Following Patrick Brontë's tactless and unsuccessful attempts to persuade three of his female acquaintances to marry him and take on the mothering of his children, his wife's sister Elizabeth Branwell reluctantly agreed to leave her beloved Cornwall and take up residence at the Haworth parsonage. Elizabeth Branwell was a severe character, ill-suited to the role thrust upon her, and her strict Calvinism has frequently been blamed for the morbid fear of damnation that dogged Anne and Branwell, her favourites, and tinged even Charlotte's view of the world. Nevertheless their Aunt Branwell also provided the Brontë girls with the model of a forceful woman, independent of mind and financially self-sufficient, who could be 'very lively and intelligent, and tilt arguments against Mr Brontë without fear' (*LL* I 112).

The Brontë daughters grew up with the expectation that they would need to earn their own living and with no encouragement to rely on the 'marriage market'. Accordingly, Charlotte was ruled by the idea of self-improvement: 'She knew that she must provide for herself, and chose her trade' (*LL* I 92). That 'choice' was, in fact, severely circumscribed because for women of the middle class the only real options at this time were marriage, dependence on the family patriarch or what Charlotte described as 'governessing slavery'.

The first step towards attaining the independence of a 'trade' came in 1824 when the four older girls were sent to a charity school for daughters of the clergy at Cowan Bridge. Charlotte was eight years old and described as 'Altogether clever for her age but know[ing] nothing systematically'.[4] Her stay at Cowan Bridge lasted less than ten months but the experience was seared in her memory and immortalised in

the depiction of Lowood school in *Jane Eyre*, a creation
which Charlotte steadfastly maintained 'was on the whole a
true picture of Lowood school as she knew it by experience'
(*LL* IV 300). It was not simply the harsh regime of the school
which so distressed Charlotte but the belief that it contributed to the deaths of her older sisters Maria and Elizabeth.
Certainly both sisters fell ill at school, where typhoid fever
raged in the early months of 1825. Maria was sent home in
February and died in May while Elizabeth left at the end of
May and died on 15 June. Charlotte and Emily, too, were
withdrawn from the school two weeks before Elizabeth's
death.

The loss of Maria in particular was a bitter one for
Charlotte. As the oldest sibling Maria had provided Charlotte
with a degree of mothering she was unlikely to receive from
her stern aunt and so with Maria's death it was as though
Charlotte was twice made motherless. In later life Charlotte
frequently spoke of her two dead sisters, characterising them
as 'wonders of talent and kindness', and in her work the
memory of Maria inspired the depiction of Helen Burns in
Jane Eyre and perhaps the spectre of loss and motherlessness
which appears repeatedly.

It was nearly six years before Charlotte left home again for
school. Those years were important for Charlotte's development as a writer for during them she began her long literary
apprenticeship, sustained by the intense and enthusiastic
collaboration of her surviving siblings. In her *History of the
Year 1829* Charlotte tells of the first plays the children wrote
together – *Young Men* in June 1826, *Our Fellows* in July 1827
and *Islanders* in December 1827. By the time she was
fourteen years old Charlotte's literary output was vast. In a
'Catalogue of My Books, with the Period of Their Comple-
tion up to August 3rd, 1830' Charlotte lists an extraordinary
array of tales, plays, poems and romances written in the
previous fifteen months, '[m]aking in the whole twenty-two
volumes', with self-conscious pride in her own authorship.

Charlotte's inordinate creativity at this time was fuelled by the wide reading that her father not merely tolerated but heartily encouraged. Through newspapers and magazines, and the discussion they stimulated, the children took a passionate interest in current political issues and figures, and in keeping with the freedom Patrick Brontë allowed his children in many ways, he exercised remarkably little censorship over the material the children read. So Charlotte was as familiar with the comedies of Shakespeare and the poetry of Byron as with *The Pilgrim's Progress* and the Bible, as entranced by her aunt's old copies of *The Lady's Magazine* as by the eagerly awaited monthly edition of *Blackwood's Magazine*, 'the most able periodical there is'.

Together the children built up an extraordinarily detailed and imaginatively populated fantasy world. Most of the creative direction came from the older pair, Charlotte and Branwell, who between them devised a world of battles, conquests and political and sexual intrigue.

With Charlotte's departure for Roe Head school in January 1831 the collaboration was interrupted, much to Charlotte's dismay. Emily and Anne took the opportunity to defect from the fantasy world of the Verdopolitan Confederacy and establish their own realm of Gondal. Emily was disenchanted with Branwell's obsession with battle and the habit of repeatedly resurrecting dead characters. Significantly, with Anne she created not a world dominated by male rogues and soldiers but a much more female-oriented realm.

Meanwhile at Roe Head Charlotte applied herself to the task of filling the gaps in her education with remarkable yet characteristic diligence: 'She always seemed to feel that a deep responsibility rested upon her; that she was an object of expense to those at home, and that she must use every moment to attain the purpose for which she was sent to school, *i.e.*, to fit herself for governess life' [author's itals] (*LL* I 94).

Charlotte's time at Miss Wooler's school also provided her

with two friendships which were to prove the most lasting of her life. The first was with Mary Taylor, a fiercely independent girl with radical views whom Charlotte described as having 'more energy and power in her nature than any ten men you can pick out in the united parishes of Birstall and Gomersal' (*LL* I 223). Her second friend Ellen Nussey was, as Charlotte conceded, 'no more than a conscientious, observant, calm, well-bred Yorkshire girl' (*LL* III 63), but she provided Charlotte with a continuing source of support and affection. Mary nourished Charlotte's ambitious, daring and rebellious nature while Ellen appealed to Charlotte's dutiful, religious self. The difference between the two friends, then, was indicative of the deep divisions in Charlotte's own character, evident, too, in her hero worship of the disciplined integrity of Wellington and the romantic abandon of Byron. It also emerged in the developing world of her fiction where her imagination was seized by the exploits of her Byronic hero the Marquis of Douro (later the Duke of Zamora), while her conscience was appeased by pitting him against his more staid and virtuous brother Lord Charles.

After eighteen months Charlotte had learned as much as Miss Wooler's school had to offer her and she returned home in July 1832 to share her knowledge with her sisters. Charlotte also spent her time at home furthering her fictional Angrian cycle, although in describing her day in letters to her schoolfriends, she made no mention of her writing, and she passed many hours copying engravings with minute exactness in the hope that by this she might become accomplished as an artist and thereby earn her living. Such painstakingly disciplined imitation may have provided Charlotte with a way to curb her increasingly wayward imagination, but the experiment was a failure and only damaged Charlotte's eyesight.

In July 1835 the children were once again 'to divide, break up, separate'. Miss Wooler had offered to take Charlotte back as an assistant teacher at Roe Head and to accept Emily as a pupil in partial payment for Charlotte's services. It was an offer Charlotte felt she could not refuse, particularly since her brother was about to set out for London to pursue his career as an artist: 'Papa would have enough to do with his limited income should Branwell be placed at the Royal Academy' (*LL* I 129).

Branwell was always the favoured child. His supposed genius was taken on trust and encouraged regardless of the consequent sacrifices required of other family members, whereas the three Brontë women were to compose their mature work in secret, unknown either to father or son, and then only after the duties of the household had been duly completed. Charlotte shared the family's great expectations for the only son: 'she, with her own enthusiasms, looked forward to what her brother's great promise and talent might effect' (*LL* I 106). It was Branwell whom Charlotte valued as her literary collaborator and to him that she addressed her weekly letter from school, 'because to you I find most to say'. It was not surprising that as the most ambitious of the sisters she would most keenly seek vicarious fulfilment through the family son but perhaps it was because she had been so willingly co-opted into the delusion of Branwell's superiority that her disgust and bitterness at his demise were most severe. Yet even after his death, when her own success as the novelist of *Jane Eyre* was much heralded, Charlotte could still write that her 'poor father naturally thought more of his *only* son than of his daughters' (*LL* II 261). Ironically, this inequity in the Brontë household may have proved liberating for the three daughters. While Branwell was paralysed by the expectations of success that weighed so heavily upon him, the Brontë women were free to produce their own work unchecked by the burden of family expectation.

Charlotte's second stay at Roe Head was less happy than the first. She was much more suited to the role of student than that of teacher. She had no particular liking for children, abhorred stupidity and was strained by the aspect of public performance required in teaching. Emily's companionship provided little solace for Charlotte, since Emily was desperately unhappy when removed from her beloved home and moors and only lasted three months at school, returning to Haworth in October. Anne took up Emily's place in the following January.

Away from the sheltered world of her home where the siblings encouraged each other in their creative fantasies, Charlotte began to doubt not simply the propriety but the morality of her imaginative world. Charlotte was playing out the fantasies of her emerging sexuality in the fictional realm of Angria and increasingly she was racked with guilt about her secret world, her 'bright, darling dream'. She wrote to Ellen repenting of 'my evil wandering thoughts, my corrupt heart, cold to the spirit and warm to the flesh' and fearing that Ellen would pity and despise her, if she knew her thoughts, 'the dreams that absorb me; and the fiery imagination that at times eats me up' (*LL* I 139). It must have seemed a bewildering portrait to Ellen who knew only the retiring, dutiful Charlotte and nothing of her imaginative release in an 'infernal world'.

Charlotte herself was shocked by the hold that the Angrian dream had on her imagination, the readiness with which her mind deserted the real world for her fantasy kingdom. Whereas her sister Emily wholeheartedly welcomed the liberation offered by her imaginative world, Charlotte was increasingly torn by the conflicting claims of reality and imagination. Nevertheless, while in some respects Charlotte may have been disturbed by her creative impulses, in others she had no intention of forsaking them. Indeed, at this time the first real indications of the depth of Charlotte's ambition as a writer began to emerge, when in the welcome break of her Christmas holiday in 1836, she took the bold step of writing to the Poet Laureate Robert Southey seeking his judgement on her poetry. Southey's reply, while gratifying in itself, might well have crushed a lesser spirit. Not only did he sound a personal note guaranteed to reverberate with her own sense of guilt – 'The day dreams in which you habitually indulge are likely to induce a distempered state of mind' (*LL* I 155) – but he enlisted the weight of general public censure against female writers: 'Literature cannot be the business of a woman's life, and it ought not to be. The more she is engaged in her proper duties, the less leisure will she have for it, even as an accomplishment and a recreation' (*LL* I 155). The fact that Charlotte replied to such admonitions is evidence of the spirit which would later declare to her publisher: 'I have my own doctrines, not acquired, but innate, some that I fear cannot be rooted up without tearing away all the soil from which they spring' (*LL* III 39). Her answer to Southey is apparently apologetic – 'I shall never more feel ambitious to see my name in print' – but with characteristic ambivalence there is an edge of self-justification in the apology:

In the evenings, I confess, I do think, but I never trouble any one else with my thoughts. I carefully avoid any appearance of preoccupation and eccentricity, which might lead those I live amongst to suspect the nature of my pursuits. Following my father's advice – who from my childhood has counselled me, just in the wise and friendly tone of your letter – I have endeavoured not only attentively to observe all the duties a woman ought to fulfil, but to feel deeply interested in them. I don't always succeed, for sometimes when I'm teaching or sewing I would rather be reading or writing; but I try to deny myself; and my father's approbation amply rewarded me for the privation. (*LL* I 157–8)

And with a determination to read in Southey's letter what she most wanted to hear, she asserted: 'You do not forbid me to write; you do not say that what I write is utterly destitute of merit. You only warn me against the folly of neglecting real duties for the sake of imaginative pleasures' (*LL* I 157).

The exchange with Southey was all too brief a diversion in the miserable grind of life as a teacher in which she 'seemed to have no interest or pleasure beyond the feeling of duty' (*LL* I 136). In the spring of 1837 Miss Wooler moved her school from the pleasant location of Roe Head to the much less healthy surroundings of Dewsbury Moor. By December Anne had fallen ill and was soon to leave. Charlotte, already feeling a 'miserable and wretched touchiness of character' and haunted by the memory of her sisters' deaths after their illnesses at Cowan Bridge, found herself in a 'regular passion', haranguing Miss Wooler for her lack of concern at Anne's condition (*LL* I 164). Such an outburst was rare for Charlotte but a capacity for passionate anger lay within her outwardly quiet nature. She ascribed a 'warm temper' to herself and yet when she claimed to be 'a passionate fool' with a humour 'too soon overthrown – too sore – too demonstrative and vehement', she was revealing more about her inner struggles than her outward demeanour (*LL* II 119). Charlotte, who later protested that 'women are supposed to be very calm generally; but women feel just as men feel' (*JE* 111), knew only too well that a demonstration of strong feeling was regarded as highly improper. On one occasion, for example, when Charlotte erupted angrily against the bigoted talk of three of her father's curates, the offenders were 'struck dumb' and her father was 'greatly horrified'.

Despite her grim determination Charlotte could not continue at Dewsbury and she left in May 1838 'a shattered wretch'. In the ensuing months she was offered a means of escape from the oppressive need to earn a living in the form of two marriage proposals – one from Henry Nussey, Ellen's brother, in February 1838 and the other from the Reverend James Bryce in August of the same year. Her refusal of both men was swift and absolute, the former because she recognised they would be ill-suited – 'I am not the serious, grave, cool-headed individual you suppose' (*LL* I 173) – and the latter because she regarded his proposal as precipitate and ridiculous. Despite her bleak prospects and another unsuccessful and unhappy attempt at governessing during the summer of 1839, Charlotte remained convinced that there was 'no more respectable character on this earth than an unmarried woman who makes her own way through life quietly perseveringly' (*LL* II 77), and she regarded women 'reared on speculation with a view to their making mercenary marriages' as 'piteously degraded' (*LL* II 221). Her determination ran counter to the prevailing assumption that 'no woman was single by choice'. Thackeray, for example, gravely underestimated the courage of her character and her dedication to her craft when he suggested in 1853 that Charlotte Brontë 'rather than have fame, rather than any other earthly good or mayhap heavenly one . . . wants some Tomkins or another to love her and be in love with . . . . here is one genius, a noble heart longing to mate itself and destined to wither away into old maidenhood with no chance to fulfil the burning desire.'[5]

The Brontë women devised a plan in the winter of 1839 which seemed to answer all their problems – Charlotte's hatred of governessing, Anne's poor health, Emily's homesickness and their abiding preoccupation with attending to their father. They would open a school at Haworth parsonage.

This desire for financial autonomy was accompanied in Charlotte by a move toward artistic independence. She was moving out of Branwell's sway, determined to renounce the private – and unpublishable – fantasies of her Angrian dream. She longed to quit 'that burning clime' and turn to 'a cooler region where the dawn breaks grey and sober' but she confessed that it was 'no easy theme to dismiss from my imagination the images which have filled it so long'.[6] In the summer of 1840 she sent Wordsworth a story she had written during the previous winter, 'a Richardsonian concern' featuring two Angrian characters, 'Messrs. Percy and West'.

Wordsworth's reply seems to have been none too en-

couraging and the plan for a school was not sufficiently
concrete to prevent Charlotte from forcing herself to seek
another position, 'though I *hate* and *abhor* the very thought of
governesship' (*LL* I 194). She took up a situation at Rawdon
in March 1841 and though it proved less miserable than her
last position, she still nourished plans to escape. In July she
was thinking in terms of setting up a school in the East
Riding, a more desirable location than Haworth, and by
October she was exhilarated by the prospect of going abroad
to study. The rationale was simple – a Continental education
would fit her better to run a school for young ladies. More
fundamentally, though, Charlotte longed to break out of her
dreary existence – 'I burn to go somewhere else' – and her
friend Mary Taylor, already studying in Brussels, offered the
encouragement Charlotte needed, 'cast[ing] oil on the
flames' (*LL* I 245). Ironically, in all of this Charlotte
resembled her father, for he too had craved learning and
raised himself from a poor Irish farm boy to a Cambridge-
educated minister of the Church of England. Indeed,
Charlotte appealed to the example of her father in pleading
with her Aunt Branwell to finance the venture: 'Papa will
perhaps think it a wild and ambitious scheme; but who ever
rose in the world without ambition? When he left Ireland to
go to Cambridge University, he was as ambitious as I am
now' (*LL* I 243).

Charlotte's determination prevailed and escorted by their
father Charlotte and Emily left England in February 1842 to
take up residence at the Pensionnat Heger in Brussels.
Charlotte relished her return to student life 'with the same
avidity that a cow, that has long been kept on dry hay, returns
to fresh grass. Don't laugh at my simile. It is natural to me to
submit, and very unnatural to command' (*LL* I 260). She
applied herself to her studies with characteristic zeal and
claimed to be 'never unhappy', despite her isolation from,
and dislike of, her Catholic, Belgian schoolfellows. Impressed by the application of the English sisters, the Hegers

offered to keep Emily and Charlotte on at the school beyond their planned date of departure in September, waiving their tuition fees in return for services as music and English teachers respectively. The plan, however, was disrupted by the death of their Aunt Branwell in October, upon which the sisters immediately returned home.

In January 1843 Charlotte returned to Brussels alone, unable to persuade Emily to leave her home for the second time. Charlotte was now to receive a salary of sixteen pounds for teaching English from which she paid ten francs a month to continue her German lessons. Her second stay at the Pensionnat Heger was much less happy. The loathsome task of teaching weighed heavily upon her and her solitude was extreme with Emily back at home and Mary Taylor having left for Germany after her younger sister Jessie died in Brussels in October 1842. In addition, Charlotte found herself increasingly infatuated with M. Heger and as a corollary her relations with Mme Heger gradually deteriorated. By the time she resolved to leave the stresses of the Pensionnat Heger she was in extremely low spirits, 'a trifle shaken' in mind. Nevertheless the Brussels experience had been one of important growth and it furnished Charlotte with much of the material she was to use in *The Professor* and *Villette*.

Charlotte's return to England did not restore her spirits as she had hoped. The tiny village of Haworth seemed dull by comparison with the 'brilliant capital' of Brussels, Charlotte sorely missed M. Heger, and despite issuing a prospectus and soliciting pupils, her plans to open a school came to nothing as no students came forward. Her dissatisfaction was exacerbated by the departure of Mary Taylor for New Zealand in March 1845. For Charlotte it was 'as if a great planet fell out of the sky'. She yearned to break away herself and entertained the idea of taking a situation in Paris. To Ellen Nussey she wrote 'I shall soon be 30 – I have done nothing yet . . . . There was a time when Haworth was a very pleasant place to me, it is not so now – I feel as if we were all buried here – I long to travel – to work to live a life of action'. She was dogged by headaches and 'sickliness', a characteristic reaction throughout her life to depression of spirits or stress. The disgrace of Branwell's dismissal from his position as a tutor at Thorp Green in July 1845 was aggravated by his impossible behaviour at home where he attempted to obliterate his misery with alcohol and drugs.

Just as the 'prospect before and behind' seemed bleakest to Charlotte, a door suddenly opened into longed-for horizons:

> One day in the autumn of 1845, I accidentally lighted on a MS. volume of verse in my sister Emily's hand-writing. Of course I was not surprised, knowing that she could and did write verse. I looked it over, and something more than surprise seized me – a deep conviction that these were not common effusions, nor at all like the poetry women generally write. I thought them condensed and terse, vigorous and genuine. To my ear they had also a peculiar music, wild, melancholy, and elevating. (*LL* II 79)

Charlotte was fired with the idea of publishing a selection of Emily's poems along with contributions from Anne and herself. Only her strong ambition enabled her to overcome Emily's staunch resistance to the idea and the repeated indifference of publishers. Finally the *Poems* of Acton, Ellis, and Currer Bell appeared in May 1846, published at the authors' expense. The choice of sexually ambiguous pseudonyms was the result of a wise reluctance to declare themselves as women: 'we had a vague impression that authoresses are liable to be looked on with prejudice; we noticed how critics sometimes use for their chastisement the weapon of personality, and for their reward a flattery which is not true praise' (*LL* II 80).

Only two copies of the *Poems* were sold, but the crucial step towards literary careers had been taken: 'the mere effort to succeed had given a wonderful zest to existence'. Since she was ignorant of how to overcome the difficulties met by unknown authors in bringing their work before the public, Charlotte appealed to Messrs Aylott and Jones, the publishers of the *Poems*, for 'any hint as to the way in which these difficulties are best met'. Demonstrating a telling combination of determination and naiveté, Charlotte sent the manuscripts from one publisher to the next, reusing the same wrapper so that it became an obvious record of previous rejections. Finally Anne's *Agnes Grey* and Emily's *Wuthering Heights* were accepted by Thomas Newby and Charlotte's novel, *The Professor*, continued on its unsuccesful way alone.

Charlotte's first novel, her 'idiot child', was never published in her lifetime. Instead, inspired by a notice of rejection which nevertheless offered encouragement and constructive criticism, Charlotte completed her next work *Jane Eyre* in August 1847 and sent it to Smith, Elder and Company, the publishers who had been so helpful on the subject of *The Professor*. It was enthusiastically accepted and ran to two editions before the year was out, quickly becoming one of the year's best sellers.

With the success of *Jane Eyre* Emily's and Anne's publisher Newby attempted to confuse the identity of the three Bells, suggesting that all three novels and Anne's forthcoming *The Tenant of Wildfell Hall* were the work of one pen. In order to still her publisher's disquiet Charlotte resolved to prove the separate identities of the Bells by presenting themselves in the London office of Smith, Elder and Company. Predictably, Emily refused to be a party to the plan.

Charlotte's visit to London in July 1848 provided her first taste of literary celebrity. The two sisters were fêted, dining with their publisher and being taken to the opera, the Royal Academy and the National Gallery. Charlotte paid for her intense excitement with the familiar headaches and sickness and she returned home a 'jaded wretch'.

Once home Charlotte took up work on the first volume of *Shirley*. However, with the fruits of celebrity scarcely tasted, she was about to endure a year of family distress which would make all thought of literary fame insignificant. As Charlotte declared in retrospect 'had a prophet warned me how I should stand in June 1849 – how stripped and bereaved – had he foretold the autumn, the winter, the spring of sickness and suffering to be gone through – I should have thought – this can never be endured' (*LL* II 340). The first blow came with Branwell's death in September 1848. The day of his funeral proved to be the last time Emily left the parsonage. She, too, sickened and with frightening stoicism died in December. With two siblings gone Charlotte noted the first signs of consumption in Anne with feelings of panic. A belated journey in search of health-giving sea air saw Anne die in Scarborough in May 1849.

Charlotte was left destitute. Her two sisters had provided not only her principal fund of emotional sustenance but also the sole source of support and judgement in her literary endeavours. With the 'two human beings who understood [her] . . . gone' Charlotte wrote with a new sense of vulnerability to her publisher as an 'author who has shewn his book to none, held no consultation about plan, subject, characters or incidents, asked and had no opinion from one living being, but fabricated it darkly in the silent workshop of his own brain' (*LL* III 21).

In this sombre mood Charlotte completed *Shirley* at the end of August 1849, deeply grateful for the occupation provided by her work: 'Lonely as I am – how should I be if Providence had never given me courage to adopt a career – perseverance to plead through two long, weary years with publishers till they admitted me? . . . As it is, something like hope and motive sustains me still. I wish all your daughters – I wish every woman in England had also a hope and motive' (*LL* III 6). Shortly after *Shirley*'s appearance in October Charlotte accepted her publisher's invitation to London. There she met Thackeray, to whom she had dedicated the second edition of *Jane Eyre*, and Harriet Martineau, the influential novelist and political economist. Charlotte now had that 'passport to the society of clever people' she hoped literary fame would bring. Sadly she no longer had her sisters to share it with and alone the ordeal of her introduction to society often seemed too daunting.

Despite her paralysing shyness, though, Charlotte was moved on her next visit to London in June 1850 to take the critic G. H. Lewes to task for his sexist criticism and to challenge Thackeray with his literary shortcomings: 'one by one the faults came into my mind and one by one I brought them out and sought some explanation or defence' (*LL* III 118).

Once home, after a brief visit to the Lake District in August where she met her future biographer Elizabeth Gaskell, Charlotte began the 'exquisitely painful and depressing' task of editing her sisters' works for reissue and composing a biographical preface 'such as might set at rest all erroneous conjectures respecting their identity' (*LL* III 157). Charlotte acted as an apologist for the 'very real power' of Emily's poetry and for *Wuthering Heights* whereas she was inclined to damn *Agnes Grey* with faint praise and dismiss *The Tenant of Wildfell Hall* as an 'entire mistake'. This 'sacred duty' performed, Charlotte sought to escape the desperate isolation of Haworth by accepting Harriet Martineau's invitation to visit Ambleside. Such invitations were a frequent occurrence now that Charlotte's reputation was established but often despite the inclination to do otherwise, she accepted very few. Most simply, fear held her back, for social contact was always a strain. More fundamentally, she saw company-seeking as weakness: 'I feel to my deep sorrow – to my humiliation – that it is not in my power to bear the canker of constant solitude'. And always there was a degree of guilt at leaving her father: 'I think if Papa continues pretty well I shall go' or 'I did not think Papa well enough to be left' became a constant refrain (*LL* III 166).

Companionship of a different kind was offered at this time

with the marriage proposal of James Taylor, a member of the Smith, Elder and Company publishing firm. If Charlotte's spirit was in some degree willing, her flesh was decidedly not: 'Now that he is away I feel far more gently towards him – it is only close by that I grow rigid – stiffening with a strange mixture of apprehension and anger' (*LL* III 222). Unable to countenance the 'pain and humiliation' of such a match, Charlotte farewelled Taylor as he left to establish the firm in India without giving him any hope of success in his quest for her hand.

Both her father and her publishers were anxious for Charlotte to produce another novel. Feeling the pressure of their expectations yet suffering from a lack of inspiration, Charlotte tried unsuccessfully to interest her publishers once more in the manuscript of *The Professor*. Then, after guiltily accepting invitations to London and to Manchester, where she stayed with the Gaskells, Charlotte settled down in the last months of 1851 to begin the difficult task of writing *Villette*, drawing in part on material from her rejected novel, *The Professor*. The endeavour proved arduous in the extreme. She felt 'such a craving for support and companionship as I cannot express' and suffered during most of the winter months from an illness, the origin of which, she acknowledged, was 'extreme and continuous depression of spirits' (*LL* III 330, 300). She recognised that her writing was therapeutic but still found that she was unable to apply herself consistently to her work: 'blank and heavy intervals still occur when power and will are at variance'.

She refused to '[run] away from home' until she completed her task and she finally finished in November 1852. When Smith, Elder and Company offered her £500 for the manuscript of *Villette*, the same price as for *Jane Eyre* and *Shirley*, Charlotte was justifiably disappointed. She contended that her 'chief regret' was 'that Papa will be disappointed' but she knew quite well that the sum was 'not quite equitable'. Curiously, in editorial matters she was stern to the point of inflexibility, yet she felt that to encroach on the 'arrangement of business' was 'stepping out of my position as an author' (*LL* IV 2). So whereas her contemporary Elizabeth Gaskell, for example, wrangled £2000 for her last novel *Wives and Daughters* in 1864 and George Eliot, with G. H. Lewes's astute assistance, negotiated a mammoth £7000 from George Smith for *Romola* in 1863, Charlotte Brontë's total literary earnings amounted to a mere £1500.

No sooner was the stress of novel-writing removed than a new trauma emerged. Arthur Nicholls, her father's curate of seven years, suddenly declared his unswerving attachment to Charlotte and proposed marriage. While Charlotte was shocked and unenthusiastic, her father was enraged. Even Charlotte recognised that Mr Brontë's agitation and anger were 'disproportionate to the occasion' and she wrote revealingly of 'Papa's vehement antipathy to the bare thought of any one thinking of me as a wife' (*LL* IV 30).

Relations between Patrick Brontë and Nicholls were so strained that Charlotte gladly escaped to London in January 1853 to deal with the proofs of her forthcoming novel. On this visit she chose to see 'the *real* [rather] than the *decorative* side of Life' – prisons, hospitals, the Bank of England and the Stock Exchange. She returned to continuing domestic tension at Haworth which was not alleviated until Nicholls left the parish in May. His departure, however, did not signal the end of relations with Charlotte. A correspondence between them, initiated by Nicholls and unknown to her father, grew and when Nicholls came to stay at nearby Oxenhope in January 1854, Charlotte saw a good deal of him. Mr Brontë finally agreed to Nicholls's return to the parish in May, his conciliatoriness no doubt aided by the unsatisfactoriness of the curate who replaced Nicholls.

With his return Nicholls's engagement to Charlotte was agreed upon. In many ways Charlotte had been won by the depth and persistence of his attachment and yet there seems something painfully subdued in the terms in which she announced her engagement. She spoke of 'esteem and if not love – at least affection' and confessed 'My destiny will not be brilliant, certainly, but Mr. Nicholls is conscientious, affectionate, pure in heart and life' (*LL* IV 116). Since the couple were to live at Haworth parsonage, the one feature of the impending marriage which Charlotte felt she could dwell on with 'unmingled satisfaction, with a *certainty* of being right' was the fact that it would take nothing away from 'the attention I owe to my Father' (*LL* IV 119).

Before the wedding Charlotte visited Elizabeth Gaskell in Manchester once more, conscious that it might be their last encounter for some time since Nicholls was unlikely to approve of Gaskell's Unitarianism. The marriage took place on 29 June 1854. Charlotte was 'given away' by her old schoolteacher Miss Wooler, since Mr Brontë did not attend the ceremony, reputedly having refused to do so at the last moment.

After a honeymoon in Ireland the couple returned to Haworth at the beginning of August. In marriage Charlotte found her life 'changed indeed' as she was caught up in the duties of a minister's wife. She found virtually no time to work on her new novel *Emma*, which exists only as a fragment. 'If you had not been with me', Thackeray reported Charlotte as saying to Nicholls one December night, 'I must have been writing now' (*P* 241). By January Charlotte was ill with 'indigestion' and continual 'faint sickness' and suspected that she was pregnant. In the ensuing weeks her nausea did not abate and she took virtually no food: 'A wren would have starved on what she ate during those last six weeks'.[7] She died on 31 March 1855 at the age of 38. The cause of death was given as consumption, although subsequently it has been the subject of considerable speculation. Dr Phillip Rhodes, for example, has asserted that the true cause was *hyperemesis gravidarum*, a 'neurotic condition' of pregnancy characterised by persistent vomiting.[8] And certainly Elizabeth Gaskell did not accept the inevitability of Charlotte's death, as she must have in the case of consumption: 'How I wish I had known! . . . I do fancy that if I had come, I could have induced her, – even though they had all felt angry with me at first, – to do what was so absolutely necessary, for her very life' [that is, presumably to take food]. More recently, however, John Maynard and Dr Gerson Weiss have questioned this diagnosis, arguing that no proof exists that Brontë was actually pregnant and that her symptoms were consistent with 'a severe terminal wasting disease'.[9]

Charlotte Brontë lived and wrote in a time of transition for women. In the literary world women were achieving unprecedented prominence, so that by 1852 G. H. Lewes could refer to the 'advent of female literature'. And in a wider sphere the beginnings of a feminist movement were evident in agitation for female suffrage, reform of the marriage laws, and expanded opportunities for women's education and employment. Yet despite the signs of change women still suffered from enormous constraints in mid-nineteenth-century England.

In the legal system, for example, the subjection of women was deeply entrenched, particularly in the marriage contract in which 'the very being or legal existence of the woman is suspended during marriage or at least incorporated and consolidated into that of the husband'.[10] In practice this meant that until 1882 a married woman could not legally hold any property in her own right, nor could she enter any legal contracts. She had no rights over her children, no claim to her independent earnings and could not leave her husband unless she obtained a legal separation, a prohibitively expensive process granted only in the case of desertion or extreme cruelty. In short, as John Stuart Mill observed in *The Subjection of Women*, 'the wife's position under the common law of England is worse than that of the slaves in the law of many countries'.[11]

The social and cultural constraints were no less damaging than the legal restrictions. As Florence Nightingale protested in 1852, women were denied satisfaction of their 'passion, intellect and moral activity', their selfhood bound and

maimed as surely as the feet of Chinese women. Voices on all
sides called for women to assume their place in the family.
So, Southey reminded Brontë of her 'proper duties', de-
creeing that literary endeavour had no rightful place in a
woman's life. And even Elizabeth Gaskell, a much more
sympathetic commentator, could not countenance the idea
that a female artist might be relieved in the name of her Art of
her 'womanly' duty:

When a man becomes an author, it is probably merely a
change of employment to him. He takes a portion of that
time which has hitherto been devoted to some other study
or pursuit, he gives up something of the legal or medical
profession . . . and another merchant or lawyer, or doctor,
steps into his vacant place, and probably does quite as well
as he. But no other can take up the quiet, regular duties of
the daughter, the wife, or the mother, as well as she whom
God has appointed to fill that particular place: a woman's
principal work in life is hardly left to her own choice; nor
can she drop the domestic charges devolving on her as an
individual, for the exercise of the most splendid talents
that were ever bestowed. And yet she must not shrink from
the extra responsibility implied by the very fact of her
possessing such talents. She must not hide her gift in a
napkin; it was meant for the use and service of others. In an
humble and faithful spirit must she labour to do what is not
impossible, or God would not have set her to do it.[12]

Just as ambition was cause for guilt in women, so too was
passion in an age which subverted and denied female
sexuality in many ways: 'Women go about maudling to each
other and preaching to their daughters that "women have no
passions"'.[13] Accordingly in fiction of the time the sexual
element of relationships is frequently evaded by the emphasis
on filial or sibling bonding between the two 'lovers'.
Similarly in the visual arts the mid-nineteenth century sees

the celebration in Pre-Raphaelite paintings of the enervation of the female form – languid women without energy and, as a corollary, without appetite. And the nineteenth-century interest in the medieval evident in Pre-Raphaelite art, the poetry of Keats, Tennyson, Patmore and Rossetti, and the prose of Ruskin and Eliza Lynn Linton all commend a chivalric code which, while it 'honours' women also objectifies them as chaste and untouchable. So John Stuart Mill protested: 'We have had the morality of submission, and the morality of chivalry and generosity; the time is now come for the morality of justice'.[14]

Charlotte Brontë was personally affected by a number of the important issues surrounding the 'Woman Question' in mid-nineteenth-century England. She speculated 'much on the existence of unmarried and never-to-be married women nowadays' (*LL* II 77) and despite her apprehensiveness of and distaste for single life, she refused to consider marriage as an escape and accorded great respect to those women who refused unsuitable marriages and worked their way through life 'quietly perseveringly'.

She felt strongly that women should be provided with the opportunities for an education and occupation to 'give their existence some object' and to enable them to escape the dependency which she saw as 'the one great curse of a single life' (*LL* III 5). At the same time, though, Charlotte stopped short of more radical solutions: 'It is true enough that the present market for female labour is quite overstocked, but where or how could another be opened? Many say that the professions now filled only by men should be open to women also; but are not their present occupants and candidates more than numerous enough to answer every demand . . . . One can see where the evil lies, but who can point out the remedy?' (*LL* II 216). With characteristic ambivalence Brontë well understood the impulse of women tried beyond patience 'at last to send up to Heaven any piercing cry for relief' (*LL* II 216) but was inclined to regard the prospects of women's practical, political advancement with a degree of quietism: 'Certainly there are evils which our own efforts will best reach; but as certainly there are other evils – deep-rooted in the foundations of the social system – which no efforts of ours can touch; of which we cannot complain; of which it is advisable not too often to think' (*LL* III 150).

Charlotte Brontë's most radical self and her most powerful contributions to the cause of women emerged in her fiction. Despite the very considerable pressures within her family and society, she never betrayed her vocation as an artist. She courageously confronted the double standards of critics who unfairly distinguished between male and female writers, wrote with 'faithful allegiance to Truth and Nature' and was liberated in her writing to demonstrate her deepest awareness of the social, intellectual and sexual inequities faced by women of her time.

2 Charlotte Brontë's Fiction

> The first duty of an author is, I conceive, a faithful allegiance to Truth and Nature; his second, such a conscientious study of Art as shall enable him to interpret eloquently and effectively the oracles delivered by those two great deities. The Bells are very sincere in their worship of Truth, and they hope to apply themselves to the consideration of Art, so as to attain one day the power of speaking the language of conviction in the accents of persuasion. (*LL* II 243)

Charlotte Brontë occupies a position of major importance in the history of women's literature. She gave a female voice to fiction, creating a new focus on woman as the central shaping consciousness of the novel. In doing so, she laid claim to unchartered territory, breaking silences, asserting truths previously unspoken and offering a new perception of reality for women.

Charlotte's literary precursors, although not so startlingly absent as her sister Emily's, are not immediately apparent. Certainly she herself disclaimed any literary debt:

> The standard heroes and heroines of novels are personages in whom I could never from childhood upwards take an interest, believe to be natural, or wish to imitate. Were I obliged to copy any former novelist, even the greatest, even Scott, in anything, I would not write. Unless I have something of my own to say, and a way of my own to say it

in, I have no business to publish. Unless I can look beyond the greatest Masters, and study Nature herself, I have no right to paint. Unless I can have the courage to use the language of Truth in preference to the jargon of Conventionality, I ought to be silent. (*LL* II 255)

Although Charlotte read widely, she held earlier English novelists in fairly low esteem. In a reading list devised for her friend Ellen in 1834, for example, she recommended lists of poets, biographers and historians but declared summarily, 'For fiction – read Scott alone; all novels after his are worthless' (*LL* I 122). Elizabeth Barrett Browning's troubled search for literary 'grandmothers' – 'For we think back through our mothers if we are women. It is useless to go to the great men writers for help, however much one may go to them for pleasure'[1] – seems not to have plagued Charlotte, who remained comparatively unimpressed by her female forbears. While she was reserved in her respect for George Sand (*LL* II 180; III 172–3), for example, she was positively hostile to Jane Austen:

She does her business of delineating the surface of the lives of genteel English people curiously well; there is a Chinese fidelity, a miniature delicacy in the painting: she ruffles her reader by nothing vehement, disturbs him by nothing profound: the Passions are perfectly unknown to her; she rejects even a speaking acquaintance with that stormy Sisterhood . . . what sees keenly, speaks aptly, moves flexibly, it suits her to study, but what throbs fast and full, though hidden, what the blood rushes through, what is the unseen seat of Life and the sentient target of death – *this* Miss Austen ignores . . . . Jane Austen was a complete and most sensible lady, but a very incomplete, and rather insensible (*not senseless*) woman, if this is heresy – I cannot help it. (*LL* III 99)

Nevertheless, it is possible to trace some points of connection between Charlotte Brontë and earlier writers. Her creation of the entrapped heroine and her lengthy internal monologues have been seen as reminiscent of Samuel Richardson.[2] Equally, the preoccupation with imprisonment and the 'extra-rational' in her novels has been linked with the Gothic novel, although Charlotte's use of Gothic device is acknowledged as having a new force – both symbolic and psychological – and integrity.[3] Walter Scott's influence is evident especially in the juvenilia with its sweep of historical romance and the contemporary influence of Thackeray can be traced in the narrative scope and voice of *Shirley*.

More generally, certain recurring concerns link Charlotte Brontë's work with what Gilbert and Gubar have suggested are prevailing preoccupations of the nineteenth-century female imagination. They argue that a distinctively female literary tradition is marked by images of enclosure and escape, fantasies in which maddened doubles function as asocial surrogates for docile selves, metaphors of physical discomfort manifested in frozen landscapes and fiery interiors and obsessive depictions of diseases like anorexia, claustrophobia, agoraphobia and myopia. Examples of such patterns abound in Charlotte Brontë's work although this can be seen as much as a response to the confinement and constraint of women in Victorian society as an indication of literary influence.

Perhaps the Brontës' most influential predecessors were not the earlier novelists but the Romantic poets. Byron loomed as the hero of Charlotte's youth and although his most decisive effect is evident in the juvenilia, his presence lingers in the creation of her heroes in the mature works. More broadly, the Romantic cult of the individual, the movement's preoccupation with the feelings, thoughts and dreams of the solitary individual, its recognition of the formative importance of childhood and its passionate study of nature and one's place in the natural world all find their way into Charlotte Brontë's fiction.

The most potent literary interaction of all was that which Charlotte enjoyed with her sisters. She wrote in close collaboration with Branwell in her youth, but it was her sisters Emily and Anne who offered Charlotte the adult literary kinship she needed. She felt that her sisters were 'the two human beings who understood [her] and whom [she] understood' and after their deaths her feeling of isolation was extreme. Less confident in her judgement and more vulnerable to criticism, she wrote the concluding sections of *Shirley* as an author 'who has shewn his book to none, held no consultation about plan, subject, character or incidents, asked and had no opinion from one living being, but fabricated it darkly in the silent workshop of his own brain' (*LL* III 21).

Beyond support, the more tangible benefits of a shared experience of authorship are evident in the improvement in *Jane Eyre* after Charlotte's first novel *The Professor*. Both Anne and Emily had completed their first novels before Charlotte wrote *Jane Eyre* and in the powerful narrative of Charlotte's heroine Jane we might see, for example, the shadow of the direct first-person narrative of Anne's *Agnes Grey* (Charlotte had no precedent for the female narrator in any of her juvenilia). And as different as *Jane Eyre* is from *Wuthering Heights*, Charlotte's novel shows signs of debt to the unashamed passion and supernatural interests of *Wuthering Heights* and to the poetic force of Emily's prose.

In the end Charlotte's literary influence on those who came after her is more significant than the debt she owed to those who went before. In a period when new heights of achievement were attained by female authors, Charlotte's authority and influence were rivalled only by George Eliot's. Indeed one contemporary, the novelist Margaret Oliphant, claimed that perhaps 'no other writer of her time has impressed her mark so clearly on contemporary literature, or drawn so many followers onto her peculiar path'.[4] The impact of *Jane Eyre* in particular was immediate. Dickens's *David Copperfield* and George Eliot's *The Mill on the Floss* both owe something to Charlotte's novel, and periodicals of the time testify to her profound influence on the conception of the Victorian heroine.

Charlotte's work provided a crucial alternative to the socially oriented, essentially conservative ethic of the prevailing middle-class novel. Fundamentally, Charlotte endorsed a fiercely individualistic self-sufficiency which placed the demands of society second to those of self, establishing a particularly important priority for women given the nature of Victorian society's demands upon them: 'If all the world hated you, and believed you wicked, when your own conscience approved you, and absolved you from guilt, you would not be without friends' (*JE* 70).

In creating her heroines Charlotte demonstrated that rebellion was necessary and just and concomitantly that it was strengthened, not weakened, by self-control. She also acknowledged the strength of female sexuality, asserted a difference between affection and passion and held out a dangerous and exciting – if somewhat problematic – ideal for female sexual fulfilment.

While her novels explored female vulnerability, fear and weakness with disturbing intensity, in the face of this they asserted nonetheless an integrity and strength of self in the heroines. Charlotte's heroines have an unshakeable instinct for survival in contrast to George Eliot's. Her rebels endure their trials to achieve a sense of wholeness or fulfilment whereas Eliot's non-conformists are either destroyed like Maggie Tulliver or sadly diminished like Romola, Dorothea and Gwendolen.

Through her heroines Charlotte highlighted perhaps more realistically than any of her contemporaries the grim economic truths faced by women seeking any kind of independence. Her aspiration towards a bourgeois ideal of economic self-sufficiency can be seen as conservative but should not be equated with conservatism in sexual politics.[5] Charlotte cherished radical notions of female independence and autonomy and she held out the possibility of a spiritual liberation in the minimal but ultimate domain for the dispossessed – an 'empire over self'.

Charlotte's innovations in the novel were triumphs both of theme and style. In her heroines she attempted to reconcile body and mind, just as in the novel form she sought to unite realism and dream, effecting the 'intersection of the romance proper and the novel proper'.[6]

Paradoxically, that fusion came from a woman whose life and work were shaped by division. Yet Charlotte's characteristic use of antithesis was by no means exclusive to her. She lived in a period much given to the construction of polarities. Matthew Arnold, for example, diagnosed the social alternatives as Culture and Anarchy in his influential book of that name in 1869 and George Eliot's first novel, *Adam Bede* (1859), defines its world through a series of opposites – Adam and Seth, Dinah and Hetty, Hayslope and Stonyshire. In an age shaken by religious, scientific and social upheaval this attraction to opposites might be seen as a longing for clarity, for the reductive certainty of black and white. For women, however, there was arguably more at stake. Division enabled the coexistence of the acquiescence that was demanded and the rebellion that was craved. Hence the prevalence of the 'maddened double' in so much women's fiction, that outlaw who could give vent to a rage prohibited in the heroine.[7] In Charlotte's work that division was manifest in various ways: in the opposition of characters – Helen and Bertha, Rochester and St John, Robert and Louis, Caroline and Shirley; in the contrast of concepts – Freedom and Duty, Reason and Feeling; and in the antithesis of states – hunger and plenty, warmth and cold.

At a more fundamental level a divisive tension exists in the prose itself. In one manifestation it takes the form of the feeling behind the prose straining against the ostensible statement. So, in its most extreme fictional example we have the creation of the unreliable narrator in Lucy Snowe or in a letter about Emily's death we find protest seething beneath avowed acceptance.[8]

> So I will not now ask why Emily was torn from us in the fulness of our attachment, rooted up in the prime of her own days, in the promise of her powers – why her existence now lies like a field of green corn trodden down – like a tree in full bearing – struck at the root; I will only say, sweet is rest after labour and calm after tempest, and repeat again and again that Emily knows that now. (*LL* II 295)

In more formal terms it affects the very structure of Charlotte's sentences which frequently use antithesis – 'As little could I fill the place of their mutual friend as that of their deadly foe: as little could I stand between them as trample over them' – and syntactic inversion: 'Motive there was none why I should try to recover or wish to live'.[9]

This preoccupation with division is for Charlotte the precondition for union – the necessary recognition of the parts that make possible the whole. The fusion is achieved in two ways – thematically in the renunciation of extremes and the attainment of balance, which forms the essential struggle of her heroines' growth to maturity, and stylistically in her use of poetic devices in prose. Charlotte's predominantly figurative language is profoundly suggestive, privileging the imaginative and intuitive ahead of the rational. Similarly her use of the supernatural reinforces the sense of knowledge beyond logic, of truths that are felt as much as thought. As in the processes of poetry, meaning is created through a complex pattern of association with the use of metaphor and symbol – the fire and moon in *Jane Eyre*, for example, or the garden in *Villette*. Recalling the Romantic poets, Charlotte demonstrates a capacity to fuse emotion and setting and her novels are marked by a striking vitality of imagery. Habits of personification, reminiscent of her childhood favourite Bunyan, enable her to externalise and visualise psychological states. In this way physical states powerfully suggest their psychological correlatives with, for example, confinement signalling oppression or hunger underscoring deprivation. In all, then, Charlotte Brontë's novels offer not just a thematic exploration of the necessary union of thought and feeling but an experience of that union as her poetic prose ensures that the reader is both intellectually and emotionally engaged.

This poetic form marked an important development in women's literature. Its focus on the imagination and exploration of a deeply subjective and intuitive female consciousness – 'what throbs fast and full, though hidden, what the blood rushes through, what is the unseen seat of Life' (*LL* III 99) – created an essentially asocial novel. Raymond Williams suggests that a central concern of the emerging English novel was 'the exploration of community' and this seems plausible for a line traced from Austen through Thackeray and Dickens to George Eliot. Charlotte Brontë, however, created a new direction, offering an important alternative to the novels of the other 'star in the firmament', George Eliot.

The concerns of both novelists were deeply moral but whereas in Eliot the imperative for women was responsibility to others, in Brontë it was responsibility to self: the gauge of spiritual health was duty and the social ethic in one, personal integrity in the other. Indeed, the 'moral' choice in Brontë was frequently antisocial, arising from the need to assert the self in a hostile environment. At various points it is a condition of growth for all Brontë's heroines that they rebel against socially prescribed duties and dictates.

Brontë's heroines all find fulfilment in partnership but an important component of their relationships is the degree of autonomy, and hence self-respect, they exercise within them. Each heroine has a deeply private creative world – Frances with her poems, Jane her paintings, Shirley her world of visions and Lucy her essays and letters – which offers a degree of spiritual autonomy. Each nourishes an intense inner life which can be oppressed by external forces but never destroyed, as Rochester recognises with mounting frustration:

> Consider that eye: consider the resolute, wild, free thing looking out of it, defying me, with more than courage – with a stern triumph. Whatever I do with its cage, I cannot get at it – the savage, beautiful creature! If I tear, if I rend the slight prison, my outrage will only let the captive loose. Conqueror I might be of the house, but the inmate would escape to heaven before I could call myself possessor of its clay dwelling-place. And it is you, spirit – with will and energy, and virtue and purity – that I want: not alone your brittle frame. (*JE* 322)

Such an inner domain is at once enormously powerful and vulnerable, as the nature of the images in the passage makes clear. That inner spiritual power needs to be extended and translated into action in the outer world and one important form of that extension is the acquisition of financial power. Even from the first in *The Professor* Frances asserts 'Think of my marrying you to be kept by you, Monsieur! I could not do it; and how dull my days would be!' (*P* 200). Jane Eyre returns to her relationship with Rochester liberated in part by her newly discovered inheritance. Shirley wields the financial power of Fieldhead and she relinquishes it as an act of grace not of compulsion: ' "Louis," she said, "would never have learned to rule, if she had not ceased to govern" ' (*S* 638). And Lucy achieves her goal of financial autonomy with the establishment of her school at Faubourg Clotilde. This feature of her heroines accords with Brontë's own sense of the importance of money and her hard-headedness about the power it bestows:

Who holds the purse will wish to be Master, Ellen; depend
on it whether man or woman – Who provides the cash will
now and then value himself (or herself) upon it – and even
in the case of ordinary minds, reproach the less wealthy
partner – besides no husband ought to be an object of
charity to his wife – as no wife to her husband. (*LL* II 106)

Most radically, Brontë claimed a sexual identity for women.
Contrary to the effacement and denial of women's sexual
identity in the fiction and society of mid-nineteenth-century
England, Brontë asserted that women not only experience
sexual desire but have a right to expect sexual fulfilment. All
the heroines enjoy combative interaction with their male
partners and although it frequently takes the form of verbal
banter, the physicality of Brontë's language makes the sexual
dynamic clear. So, she writes in *The Professor*, for example,
of the debate 'working up the subdued excitement' or of the
confrontation between Jane and Rochester as 'perilous; but
not without its charm: such as an Indian, perhaps, feels when
he slips over the rapid in his canoe' (*JE* 306). Jane Eyre
asserts the claims of her sexuality when she refuses St John
because she cannot 'endure all the forms of love' (*JE* 410) in
marriage to him and Shirley does likewise when she insists
upon her right to choose her own partner. She makes a vital
distinction when her enraged uncle demands, 'Are you a
young lady?' and she replies 'I am a thousand times better: I
am an honest woman, and as such I will be treated' (*S* 556).

It is in the area of female sexuality, however, that Brontë's
treatment of her heroines is in some senses problematic. Her
novels are fraught with tension between a female independence of spirit and action and a feminine dependence in love
relationships.

Brontë's ambivalence is evident, too, in the creation of her
heroes. They are consistently represented as masters with the
women frequently adopting correspondingly subservient
positions. Shirley declares, for example, that she 'will accept

no hand which cannot hold me in check' (*S* 551) and Frances and Jane habitually address their partners as 'master'. The master/servant relationship is compounded by a coexisting teacher/pupil relationship with the males as the custodians of learning, dispensing knowledge and selecting books from the libraries they frequently control. Furthermore the heroines often respond in a disturbingly masochistic way to masculine aggression. Jane and Lucy feel at their ease with the rudeness of Rochester and Paul and Frances in agreeing to marry Crimsworth expresses the wish that he always remain 'un peu entêté, exigeant, volontaire' (*P* 198).

At the same time, though, there are impulses in Brontë's fiction which militate against this inequity. She adopts various strategies, for example, for containing or placing the idea of male mastery. So, Frances's speech against masculine tyranny tempers any sense of slavish obedience in her nature:

> I should have tried to endure the evil or cure it for a while; and when I found it intolerable and incurable, I should have left my torturer suddenly and silently. . . . Monsieur, if a wife's nature loathes that of the man she is wedded to, marriage must be slavery. Against slavery all right thinkers revolt, and though torture be the price of resistance, torture must be dared. (*P* 226)

Placed in the middle of an account of their domestic bliss, Frances's speech does have the aspect of a set piece, a relatively crude signal of equality and mutuality in the relationship. However in *Jane Eyre* Brontë makes a more extended attempt to envisage an equal relationship with the mutual dependence of the protagonists and in *Shirley* she endeavours to balance the notion of Louis as Shirley's 'master' and 'keeper' with the sense of Shirley as Louis's 'sovereign' and 'wily, tameless' pantheress.

Further, the teacher/pupil relationship while mirroring other inequalities of power actually carries within it the potential for equality. Of its nature it ensures that the teacher shares knowledge, the dispossessed becomes the possessed and, as happens with both Frances and Lucy, the pupil can become the teacher.

Similarly Brontë's attraction to the intemperate Byronic hero is tempered by her inclination to feminise her heroes, stressing their 'feminine' or androgynous qualities and challenging in various ways a stereotype of masculinity. And without denying the disturbing element in the heroines' responsiveness to male aggression in a paradoxical way that masculine repressiveness proves liberating for Brontë's women. The male abruptness and bullying represents a breach of decorum and convention which enables a corres-ponding freedom of expression in return. Thus Brontë's heroines acquire a remarkable capacity for frankness, as Jane Eyre explains: 'If he had been polite I would have felt constricted. But since he was rude I felt under no obligation'.

Nevertheless, Charlotte Brontë's assertiveness in the treat-ment of female sexuality is qualified by a sense of threat. Males are seen as foreign, both literally and figuratively, and her heroines are dogged by an anxiety about the loss of self involved in sexual relationships. The two aspects of assertion and threat are held together in her use of the metaphor of a precious inner space, which gives a pervasive presence to female sexuality in the novels but in the terms in which she uses it, also highlights a vulnerability to violation.[10]

It is as foolish to deny Charlotte's ambivalence in her treatment of female sexuality in the name of a feminist orthodoxy as it is absurdly ahistorical to brand her works as sexist and regressive.[11] In her novels Brontë gave women a new voice and a new place in English fiction and through them she exercised a formative influence on the women's literature that was to follow.

3 *The Professor*

In delineating male character I labour under disadvantages: intuition and theory will not always adequately supply the place of observation and experience. When I write about women I am sure of my ground – in the other case, I am not so sure. (*LL* II 312)

In 1839 at the age of 22 Charlotte Brontë resolved to forsake the imaginative world of Angria:

Yet do not urge me too fast reader: it is not easy to dismiss from my imagination the images which have filled it so long. . . . Still, I long to quit for awhile that burning clime where we have sojourned too long – its skies flame – the glow of sunset is always upon it – the mind would cease from excitement and turn now to a cooler region where the dawn breaks grey and sober, and the coming day for a time at least is subdued by clouds.[1]

Her 'Farewell to Angria' signalled the beginning of a struggle to renounce the excesses of romantic and sexual fantasy in the tales which culminated in the production of her first novel, *The Professor*, in 1846. By this time she claimed to have outgrown 'any such taste as I might once have had for ornamented or redundant composition' and to have created a hero who 'should work his way through life as I had seen real living men work theirs'.[2]

In writing *The Professor* Charlotte sought to achieve acceptance of two kinds – external acclaim as a published novelist and inner peace of mind in the face of the guilt she felt about her imaginative life.[3] In simple terms she failed on both counts for *The Professor* was not published in her lifetime and her sexual fantasies were never entirely eradicated from her fiction. Parodoxically, though, these failures contributed to her later success. The novel's repeated rejection by publishers led Charlotte to question the wisdom of her rather sterile adherence to the 'plain and homely' in *The Professor* and prompted the artistic liberation of 'something more imaginative and poetical' in *Jane Eyre*. And the determination to repress her sexual fantasy arguably brought to the foreground the whole issue of repression, providing a central subject and creative focus in her fiction.

As a transitional work *The Professor* represented an important development on the earlier fiction and anticipated much that was to come. In the figure of William Crimsworth Brontë greatly extended the role of the narrator as central protagonist and thus the possibility (if not the achievement in *The Professor*) for emotional, psychological and moral insights. In William's story, too, Brontë touched upon many of the major themes that were to occupy her creative life – the 'plain' hero/heroine; the outsider proving him/her self intellectually, spiritually and sexually; the importance of wholeness and truth to self, and the related concept of androgyny; the threat of loneliness and isolation; the opposition of Reason and Feeling, Duty and Liberty; the virtue of patience balanced against rebellion; the master/pupil relationship where 'in proportion as [the male] grew austere and magisterial, [the female] became easy and self-possessed' (121); the importance of equality in sexual partnership; the social and sexual role of women.

Brontë's choice of a male narrator is not in itself surprising. Such a device offered her the opportunity of achieving a degree of detachment in the fictional scrutiny of aspects of her relationship with M. Heger and just as importantly to disguise the story's relation to her life. (Charlotte's anxiety to avoid any recognition of the origins of the story from the Hegers is evident in her request that *Villette*, a more accurate parallel, not be published in French.) More broadly, a male narrator offered the security of assuming a 'masculine' authority in this first attempt to present herself before an unknown and unknowing readership. Indeed, Helene Moglen argues that since Brontë never encountered 'a "heroine" in her personal, cultural or political experience – or, for that matter, in literature – it was difficult for her to conceive of any woman as the focus of a work of fiction'.[4]

Nevertheless, the device created many more problems than it solved. As with Gilbert Markham in Anne Brontë's *The Tenant of Wildfell Hall*, the masculine perception of Crimsworth in *The Professor* is too often implausible, particularly in its detailed acquaintance with feminine minutiae. Both sisters try too hard to underscore the maleness of their narrator. In *The Professor* this strain is obvious from the outset in the letter which opens the novel. Striving for authenticity, it offers a succession of 'masculine' touchstones – education at Eton, an awkward incorporation of classical reference: 'certainly I never experienced anything of the Pylades and Orestes sentiment for you' (1) and a certain swaggering tone: 'you shall hear, if you choose to listen, how the world has wagged with me' (1).

Similarly, Charlotte's minor male characters are stereotyped, with Edward presented as an irredeemably wicked, heartless industrialist who whips his horse mercilessly and later beats his wife, and Pelet as a scheming, licentious foreigner, a two-dimensional character from a French farce. Charlotte's attempt to create highly charged scenes of masculine confrontation fail dismally. The clash between William and his brother Edward is marred by stilted dialogue:

'Down with your whip!' said I, 'and explain this instant what you mean.'
'Sirrah! to whom are you speaking?'
'To you. There is no one else present, I think. You say I

have been calumniating you – complaining of your low wages and bad treatment. Give your grounds for these assertions.' (35)

and Crimsworth's tussle with Hunsden quickly degenerates into bathos:

> 'Just let go my collar, Hunsden'.
> On the contrary, he swayed me to and fro; so I grappled him round the waist. It was dark; the street lonely and lampless. We had then a tug for it; and after we had both rolled on the pavement, and with difficulty picked ourselves up, we agreed to walk on more soberly. (215)

More importantly in terms of the overall achievement of the novel, Charlotte fails to offer any real understanding of her male protagonist's behaviour, where she so clearly has the opportunities to do so. Vagaries of temper which seem acceptable when viewed externally, as in the case of M. Paul in *Villette*, cause frustration and dissatisfaction with the narrative in *The Professor*. So, what appears enigmatic in M. Paul seems unselfknowing in Crimsworth. And concomitantly, the masculine narrative denies us insight into Frances, who is in many ways a more appropriate centre of interest in the novel.

Indeed, it is already clear at this early stage that Charlotte Brontë is creatively drawn towards identification with the female figure. In this respect Crimsworth represents something of a compromise – his 'masculine' authority is tempered and informed by distinctly 'feminine' characteristics and experience. A tension is evident in the novel's opening between the desire to establish Crimsworth's male *bona fides* and the wish to emphasise his atypical status as a man:

> I soon saw also that there was more than girlish – a somewhat infantine expression in her by no means small

features; this lisp and expression were, I have no doubt, a charm in Edward's eyes, and would be so to those of most men, but they were not to mine. I sought her eye, desirous to read there the intelligence which I could not discern in her face or hear in her conversation; it was merry, rather small; by turns I saw vivacity, vanity, coquetry, look out through its irid, but I watched in vain for a glimpse of soul.

(7)

In the early part of the novel Crimsworth is 'feminized' by the stress on his physical characteristics and the description of his circumstances. Smaller than his brother, for example, he feels himself to be the 'greatly inferior . . . animal' (11). He is, like his creator, short-sighted and 'always speak[s] quietly' (14). He strongly identifies with his mother, whom he resembles. So, he is drawn to her treasured portrait, while he almost fails to recognise his father's: 'The gentleman was in the shade. I could not see him well' (8). He is orphaned and displaced, shunned by male worlds of power first in the form of his aristocratic uncles and then of his mercantile brother. He experiences the powerlessness of dependence, having his talents and knowledge devalued and effaced: 'What can you do? Do you know anything besides that useless trash of college learning – Greek, Latin, and so forth?' (13). In his exclusion from his brother's milieu he recognises the feminine component of his experience in which he is 'kept down like some desolate tutor or governess' (17). Adopting the mode of a victim, he is passive in his relief that he 'had not forced circumstances; circumstances had freed me' (37) and cautious in his unwillingness to 'advance a step before [he knows] every inch of the way' (43). Even after he is 'freed' by circumstance, he is forced to 'seek another service' and 'resume the fetters of dependency' (48).

Charlotte's designation of her protagonist as 'feminine', especially in his powerlessness, foreshadows her more detailed exploration in *Shirley* of the notion of gender as socially

constructed.[5] In *The Professor*, however, whatever Crimsworth's difference from other men, his maleness gives him
access to privilege and power denied to women, and through
his character we get a revealing insight into Charlotte
Brontë's sense of sexual politics and the masculine world.

Crimsworth's initial powerlessness is reversed in every
sphere – intellectually, financially, sexually – and he achieves
kinds of power that Frances or Lucy, his female counterpart
in *Villette*, never can. This inequity emerges clearly from a
comparison of the accounts of Lucy's and Crimsworth's
journeys from England to Brussels. Crimsworth arrives
speaking the language of the country, a letter of introduction
in his pocket operating as a passport to masculine preserves
of power, feeling like a 'free, independent traveller'. His ease
with the practicalities of the journey is evidenced by the lack
of detail beyond the reported exhilaration of the 'morning
traveller who doubts not that from the hill he is ascending he
shall behold a glorious sunrise' (46). Lucy, in contrast,
obsessively details her fearful channel crossing during which
she is cheated and treated with disdain. She feels over-
whelmingly insecure in a foreign land, unable to speak the
language and unsure of its mores. The parallels are clearly
drawn – culturally dispossessed, she is deprived of her
luggage; displaced, she has nowhere to go and becomes lost;
vulnerable, she is pursued through the night streets by two
men, 'my dreaded hunters' (56).

Crimsworth's acquisition of financial security and intellectual respect with the progress of his career on the Continent
are conventional elements in a personal success story. His
sexual development, however, is more complex and revealing. In England, Crimsworth is a sexual nonentity, ignored
and excluded: 'Many smiling and graceful figures glided past
me, but the smiles were lavished on other eyes, the figures
sustained by other hands than mine. I turned away tantal-
ised' (17). Subsequently he is in danger of becoming Zoraïde
Reuter's sexual victim. The nature of the images describing

their early encounters cast Zoraïde as the aggressor. Thus she hopes to find 'some chink, some niche, where she could put in her little firm foot and stand upon my neck' (76). The sexual roles seem even more strikingly reversed in the image of the intimate inner space discovered by Zoraïde's persever- ance and manipulation: 'her finger, essaying, proving every atom of the casket, touched its secret spring, and for a moment the lid sprung open; she laid her hand on the jewel within' (90).

However, Zoraïde's triumph is only momentary. Her desire for power remains a 'hope', never realised. In this it resembles other manifestations of female sexual power in the novel. Frances's supremacy is always fleeting, lapsing char- acteristically and reassuringly back into subservience to- wards her 'maître'. The reversal of roles suggested by the 'travesty of the Moor and his gentle lady' (214) in which Desdemona smothers Othello is fantasy, the product of Hunsden's imagination, just as the figure of Lucia 'who once wore chains and broke them' (231) is a product of Frances's.

Zoraïde Reuter's position in relation to Crimsworth is bolstered initially by her economic power as his employer. Once she falls in love with him, however, the contest – 'a regular drawn battle' – is shifted to new ground and in a realm of sexual politics she is inevitably disadvantaged. Crimsworth acknowledges that he is 'changed' by the recognition of his power to 'impress' (182). He becomes despotic in the face of Zoraïde's 'slavish homage' and assumes the role of aggressor: 'meeting her gaze full, arresting, fixing her glance, I shot into her eyes, from my own, a look where there was no respect, no love, no tenderness, no gallantry; where the strictest analysis could detect nothing but scorn, hardihood, irony. I made her bear it, and feel it' (98).

Given the opportunity to exercise a double power both as teacher and male in the classroom, Crimsworth is similarly ruthless. He offers his male pupils 'but one alternative –

submission and acknowledgment of error, or ignominious
expulsion' (56) and he uses humiliation as his most powerful
disciplinary weapon with his female pupils. When Frances
enters his class as a new pupil, he is 'relentless' to the point of
sadism: 'She looked at me; her eye said most plainly, "I
cannot follow you." I disregarded her appeal, and, carelessly
leaning back in my chair, glancing from time to time with a
nonchalant air out of the window, I dictated a little faster'
(108).

Crimsworth is no wicked usurper of power. The privileges
he enjoys are no more than those conceived of by his society
as his masculine birthright. What is more telling, however, is
the fact that he jealously holds onto his power, unwilling to
relinquish the advantages it provides. He consistently defines himself as Frances's 'master' even after she has left the
school and found a job and he remains unemployed, and he
sees himself similarly as the 'gardener' with Frances his
'precious plant'. He prides himself on his capacity to waken
'pleasurable dread' (166) in Frances and his ability to control
her: 'Be as you always are. . . . you know that few could rule
her as you do' (177). In his relationship with Frances he
insists that she speak English, devising 'many a punishment'
for her 'wilfulness' in persisting with French, her most
natural language. Literally and figuratively Frances, like
Lucy in *Villette*, must speak the other's language.

In many ways, then, Brontë's 'atypical' male is all too
typical, wielding power he has not earned and participating
in sexual games that he ostensibly eschews. He is vehement
in his condemnation of 'mere licentiousness', avowedly
hating Pelet's 'fashion of mentioning love' (59), and he insists
that his modes are different and superior: 'I loved her as she
stood there, penniless and parentless; for the sensualist
charmless, for me a treasure' (149). Yet from the outset his
voyeurism – 'longing to tear . . . away' the boards that
prohibit his view of the 'consecrated ground' of Zoraïde
Reuter's pensionnat de demoiselles – demonstrates that he is

not immune to the preoccupations of the 'sensualist'. In fact, his imagination is deeply engaged with his own 'romantic visions' of the forbidden garden and he becomes caught up in the sexual milieu of the two schools. When invited to take tea with the ageing Madame Pelet, for example, his 'excited imagination' causes him to break out in a 'cold sweat' at the absurd notion that the old woman is 'going to make love' to him (60).

In his relations with Zoraïde Crimsworth takes a certain relish in sexual game-playing and even after he becomes disaffected he continues in his blunt-speaking to her because he perceives the habit 'fascinated her' (137). Before he rather primly decides that Pelet is endeavouring 'to excite ideas and wishes in my mind alien to what was right and honourable' (82) Crimsworth participates at length in the banter physically dissecting Zoraïde. He contemplates the prospect of confronting the classroom of young women with mounting excitement and once his fantasies have been shattered by the behaviour of the girls, his negative judgements are still expressed in sexually charged terms. In a particularly distasteful sequence Crimsworth describes his pupils with an obsessive physicality which suggests a deep-rooted disgust: 'her neck is grey for want of washing, and her hair so glossy with gum and grease, is not such as one feels tempted to pass the hand over, much less to run the fingers through' (85). Yet when the girls show any sign of participating in the prevailing sexual ambience Crimsworth condemns their behaviour as 'conceited coquetry and futile flirtation' and 'precocious impurity'.

Crimsworth does make some gestures at admitting his own double standards – 'I had ever hated a tyrant; and, behold, the possession of a slave, self-given, went near to transform me into what I abhorred!' (162) – but he persists nonetheless in distancing himself from passionate feeling, characterising it as alien, the province of 'mentally depraved' Belgian schoolgirls, precociously impure Catholic minds or morally

lax Frenchmen. Revealingly Crimsworth describes even his
own passions in terms of foreignness – 'I am no Oriental' (7);
'I felt at once barbarous and sensual as a pasha' (162) – almost
as though he is alienated from those aspects of himself.

Crimsworth's discomfort with passionate feeling frequently
leads to a repressiveness, especially in relation to Frances.
His pride in his own capacity to disguise his emotions and
keep his feelings disciplined by a 'silent system' (141) is
matched by his valuing of restraint in Frances. Crimsworth's
approving descriptions stress the non-sexual aspects of his
partner. Her dress during their courtship is 'rather conven-
tual' in its 'grave simplicity'; her language is 'chaste' with a
'pure and polished' accent; her room is proof against excess
in its extreme neatness and smallness, contrasting markedly
with the ornate abundance of Zoraïde's salon with its gilt
frame and gilt pendule, mirrors, and 'large lustre pendent
from the centre of the ceiling' (66). Similarly, the fire, which
is used as an extended metaphor in the novel to indicate
sexual appetite, is suitably modest and well-tended in
Frances's room. The proposal scene takes place in 'tranquil'
firelight which Crimsworth longs to control – to have 'the
power, to shovel coals into that grate *ad libitum*' (158).
Frances exists as Crimsworth's 'ideal' in so far as she is the
'personification of discretion and forethought, of diligence
and perseverance, of self-denial and self-control' (149). He
acknowledges the existence of deep feeling in Frances but he
does so in language that repeatedly emphasises not passion
but restraint:

> . . . *silent* possessor of a well of tenderness, of a flame, as
> genial as *still*, as *pure* as quenchless, of natural feeling,
> natural passion – those sources of refreshment and comfort
> to the sanctuary of home. I knew how *quietly* and how
> deeply the well bubbled in her heart; I knew how the more
> dangerous flame *burned safely* under the eye of reason [my
> italics]. (149)

It is difficult to separate the narrator from the creator in this repressive impulse for in many ways the depiction of Crimsworth's and Frances's relationship seems marked by Charlotte's determination to exorcise her guilt at the indulgence of her earlier romantic fantasies. So for example, Charlotte names the street on which Frances lives Rue Notre Dame aux Neiges with all its connotations of chill and chastity.

Crimsworth's conception of Frances as chaste, girlish and restrained obviates the threat he feels in the face of women like Zoraïde Reuter and the figure of Hypochondria, the nightmarish personification of female sexuality which appears to him as though in reaction against the relationship he finally has within his grasp. Negative images of the female form abound, too, in his descriptions of his pupils, of Madame Pelet, 'ugly, as only continental old women can be' (59) or of the 'withered old maid's carcase' (193). Likewise, sexual interaction is variously described as pouncing, attacking, conquering and controlling.

Frances's tears on the day of the wedding go unexplained, but perhaps that sombre element is not misplaced. The proposal scene is disturbing given Frances's first response on being urged to speak: 'Monsieur, vous me faîtes mal; de grâce lâchez un peu ma main droite' (197), and the image Crimsworth offers of his betrothed as being 'as stirless in her happiness as a mouse in its terror' (199). This somewhat threatening air lingers, too, in Crimsworth's attitude to his son Victor, who in his 'electrical ardour' seems especially bonded to his mother: 'Hunsden calls it his spirit, and says it should not be curbed. I call it the leaven of the offending Adam, and consider that it should be, if not *whipped* out of him, at least soundly disciplined' (235).

The more disturbing elements of the novel are not confronted in the book's conclusion. The work demonstrates the beginnings of Brontë's conviction of the need for equality and respect between men and women and in the account of the arrangements of Crimsworth's and Frances's respective schools Brontë gestures at an ideal of mutuality. However at this stage of her career the tensions that exist within characters appear as fragmentation, not as duality.

This is evident in the discrepancy between Crimsworth's theory as the self-proclaimed exceptional male and his practice as a ruthless and repressive participant in the sexual politics of the novel. This fragmentation is even more marked in the character of Frances, 'a curious mixture of tractability and firmness' (219). On the one hand Frances is given to 'gentle homage', obedience to her 'master' and servility. On the other hand she is remarkably self-assured in her creative talent (120), possessed of a 'dragon within' (229) and resolute in her commitment to financial independence (199) and marriage law justice (226).

Nonetheless Brontë makes no real attempt at synthesis, at reconciling conflicting awareness or, most importantly, at seeing the conflict as a conscious dilemma for the heroine. Rather Frances exists as a split character, in accordance with Crimsworth's perception that he has 'two wives'. Her strength and rebelliousness are merely sporadic, existing as a 'flash of eccentric vigour' (210) or like a 'white demon . . . while it lasted' (224). These are discreet moments which do not inform – or transform – the rest of Frances's life.

Crimsworth may take pride in his 'wild fruit' (183) but he is titillated rather than challenged by Frances's ardent strength. He is 'thrilled' by eliciting her defiance (156) or calculatedly provoking a demonstration of her 'wild vigour' (227), but the key to his happiness lies in his certainty of control. Sexless or passionate, Frances must be his marionette: his restraint is 'gentle enough, so long as no opposition tightened it' (199). The 'lady directress' is tolerable because she vanishes on cue at 6.00 p.m. and is 'magically restored' as his 'own little lace-mender' (223) whose joy it is to make him 'still the master in all things' (223). Clearly Frances can never evolve beyond the 'submissive and supplicating little mortal woman' so long as her strength is so erratic and devalued in the characterisation of it as somehow unreal – the manifestation of a 'sprite', an 'elf', a 'fairy' (224).

A glimmering of recognitions that are to make Charlotte Brontë such a powerful advocate for sexual equality exists in *The Professor*. However for a more sustained exploration of balance and integration we must look to the mythic simplicity and strong female voice of *Jane Eyre*.

4 *Jane Eyre*

> I know no medium: I never in my life have known any
> medium in my dealings with positive, hard characters,
> antagonistic to my own, between absolute submission and
> determined revolt. (*JE* 405)

Jane Eyre, Charlotte Brontë's first published novel, was her
most successful work and has remained the most popular of
her books. Its attractions are not difficult to isolate. The
work has a fable-like quality, depicting the personal pilgrim-
age of a heroine whose struggles for survival and justice are
essentially no less relevant for women today than for those
who received the novel with excitement in 1847. It is in many
respects Brontë's most complete novel, controlled and
manageable in ways that her later works are not. It has a
fundamental simplicity which led Charlotte's valued friend
Mary Taylor to deem it 'so perfect a work of art'.

In *Jane Eyre* Brontë's heroine has two crucial lessons to
learn in her growth towards maturity – lessons of self-control
and self-assertion. Jane's survival depends on her ability to
mediate between the potentially destructive extremes of her
own character – between the poles of Reason and Feeling,
'absolute submission and determined revolt'. Jane must
attain a form of self-control which involves not mere
repression but a complex balance of impulses in a fundamental truth to self.

The opening chapters symbolically suggest these extremes
of character. In her retreat from the drawing room to the
window seat of the breakfast room Jane finds herself
'shrined' with scarlet drapery on her right hand and on her
left the cold, drear November day beyond the glass panes

which protect but do not separate her from the winter scene. This pattern of red and white is repeated in her confinement in the red room. Its red drapery and carpet and contrasting stark white bed and easy chair embody two separate threats to Jane – a prison of passion and a chill, 'pale throne' of repression. The novel explores these polarities further in a series of antithetical figures who compete for Jane's allegiance. Most markedly, the self-immolating submission of Helen Burns contrasts with the abandoned rebellion of Bertha Mason and the passionate vehemence of Rochester is opposed to the frigid rationality of St John.

Only after Jane has negotiated some kind of personal balance can she proceed with the necessary strength to act upon the forces that oppress her, becoming agent not victim. At the heart of Jane's inner and outer struggles lies her refusal to allow her own victimisation. Jane learns the tremendous power of no-saying both as an act of resistance against oppression and as an act of self-confirmation, asserting the right to value her well-being above the demands made by others. Indeed, it is this recognition which contributes to making Jane Eyre such a potent heroine for female readers.

Jane's 'autobiography' begins significantly with her first moment of rebellion. During the previous nine unrecorded years of Jane's life she has been, according to Mrs Reed's recollection, 'patient and quiescent under any treatment'.[1] In the opening pages Jane stands before her tyrannical cousin '[h]abitually obedient', intent on 'how to endure the blow which would certainly follow the insult' (10). On this occasion reading is Jane's crime. John Reed asserts that she has 'no business to take our books' (11) and he is in fact right to sense the danger of allowing her access to his bookshelves. Knowledge gives power and in the confrontation that follows Jane turns her learning against her cousin: 'you are like the Roman emperors!' (11). Because she has 'drawn parallels', Jane can in some ways escape the paralysing isolation of her position by placing her suffering in an historical context and seeing herself 'like any other rebel slave' (12). She is inspired to revise her own history in a 'rapid rush of retrospective thought. . . . Why was I always suffering, always brow-beaten, always accused, for ever condemned?' (15). In this respect, then, it is little wonder that *Jane Eyre* alarmed some contemporary critics, for here was a subversive book pro-claiming in its opening pages the dangerous power of reading.

Jane's sudden eruption against John Reed is instinctive not chosen, the result of utter desperation. However that 'moment's mutiny' opens up a new way of seeing the world for Jane, who realises for the first time that she has choices to make and that even in a situation of virtual powerlessness she is not necessarily condemned to a passive betrayal of self.

Accordingly, in Chapter 4 when Mrs Reed misrepresents Jane to Mr Brocklehurst, obliterating any hope Jane has for a new life at school, Jane gives vent to her deep resentment. This time she acts not on instinct but on calculation: 'I gathered my energies and launched them' (36). It proves a heady experience as Jane feels the exhilaration of rebellion and righteous anger: 'my soul began to expand, to exult, with the strangest sense of freedom, of triumph, I ever felt. It seemed as if an invisible bond had burst, and that I struggled out into unhoped-for liberty' (37). However Brontë makes it clear that Jane's 'first victory' is a perilous and partial triumph. She stresses the extremity of Jane's wild responses. Her excitement is 'ungovernable', her feelings 'uncontrol-led', her conduct 'madness'. And after the first 'warm and racy' draught of vengeance, Jane is left with 'its after-flavour metallic and corroding' and 'a sensation as if I had been poisoned' (38). As though striving for equilibrium Jane seeks relief after her passionate outburst in the cold, snowy outdoors.

Without direction and control Jane's feelings are potenti-ally self-destructive. Not only is she liable to 'the pang of remorse' but under the 'agonizing stimulus' of her 'insup-portable oppression' Jane is in danger of seizing upon the only form of power readily available to the powerless – that of self-annihilation. Her ordeal in the red room ends with Jane's unconsciousness – a moment of collapse reminiscent of the frequent breakdown of Victorian heroines. Undoubtedly such breakdown is used at times as a convenient literary device but it can also be seen as the logical end to a sequence of stress and pain in which the sufferer is necessarily passive, allowing for the ultimate withdrawal into complete passivity.

Earlier, locked in the red room Jane contemplates 'never eating or drinking more, and letting myself die' (15). Self-starvation has long been the particular recourse of women in life as in literature. Emily Brontë's heroine, Catherine Earnshaw, contributes to her own death in such a manner and a refusal to eat seems to have played a part in both Emily's and Charlotte's own deaths. Beyond a minimal seizure of power, the refusal of food has a complex symbolic force for women. It can be understood as a refusal to enter into any intercourse with one's jailor or oppressor, with all the sexual ramifications of refusal of bodily invasion. It can also be viewed as a protest against the lack of emotional, intellectual and spiritual nourishment suffered by women or, paradoxically, as a perverse refusal to nourish the self – a refusal of the role of nourisher so often required of women. Certainly there are signs of Jane Eyre's refusal of such a role in her dreams of being burdened by a wailing infant which she drops in her quest to reach the distant Rochester.

Jane's trials at Gateshead are distinctly those of a woman, mirroring as they do a wider female oppression. She suffers violence at the hands of John Reed, who continually 'bullied and punished' (10), and of Mrs Reed, who attempts to crush Jane's rebellion by boxing her ears and shaking her soundly. She is repeatedly confined, most dramatically when locked in the red room where Bessie threatens further to tie her to a chair. Her powerlessness is exacerbated by her economic dependence in a household where she is 'less than a servant' (12). As 'a discord' at Gateshead she is banished from the warmth of the hearth and family intercourse and suffers the twin deprivation of hunger and cold. She is exhorted to 'remain silent' (8) and 'sit still' (12) and her aunt stipulates that it is 'only on condition of perfect submission and stillness' (18) that Jane shall be liberated from the red room. She is outcast because of her passion and 'repulsive' violence. In all, Jane is confronted by an array of repression which a great many Victorian women might have recognised as dreadfully familiar.

Jane's desire 'to achieve escape from insupportable oppression' (15) is suggested by her frequent movement towards the window, which opens out into a space not controlled by her oppressors. In one sense Jane's early rebellion facilitates her escape since it provokes her expulsion. In another, though, when Jane declares 'I can never get away from Gateshead till I am a woman' (24), the child's pragmatism masks a deeper figurative truth. Jane must attain a mature selfhood if she is ever to conquer both the internalised and the external forms of oppression operating at Gateshead.

Lowood is the first step on her path. It provides Jane with three things vital to her growth – education, love and the example of alternative forms of behaviour in the endurance of Helen Burns and the controlled rebellion of Miss Temple.

Education is the most important means of escaping the thrall of dependence for Jane, as it was for the Brontë sisters themselves and for the many middle-class women who shared with them the necessity and desire to achieve financial autonomy. Jane concludes her eight years at Lowood with marketable skills: 'qualified to teach the usual branches of a good English education, together with French, Drawing, and Music' (88). No longer 'less than a servant' Jane can shape her own future and choose to move from Lowood in marked contrast to her entrapment at Gateshead. In her time as a student Jane proves herself to be a zealous learner, seizing with both hands the 'advantages offered' and experiencing the ego-reinforcing satisfaction of achievement: 'I rose to be the first girl of the first class; then I was invested with the office of teacher' (84).

At Lowood Jane's intellectual growth is matched by an emotional growth which is no less important for her well-being. For the first time she encounters the sustaining power of love, which is given physical expression in the ways both Miss Temple and Helen Burns offer Jane warmth and nourishment. Miss Temple, for example, orders a lunch of bread and cheese for the girls after the inedible breakfast of burnt porridge just as she later shares her seedcake with Jane and Helen. In Miss Temple's room Jane finds the warmth of 'a good fire' in contrast to the raw chill of the rest of Mr Brocklehurst's establishment. Similarly, Helen Burns brings Jane coffee and bread after her ordeal standing on the stool disgraced by Brocklehurst's accusations, just as she offers spiritual nourishment 'impart[ing] strength' to Jane in her trials. Helen's and Jane's relationship is marked, too, by a physical intimacy which underscores Jane's craving for nurture. Together, then, Miss Temple and Helen assuage the cold and hunger from which Jane fears she will 'perish' in her first days at Lowood.

Paradoxically Jane must also learn to live without love but that lesson can only follow the liberating and enabling recognition of her own worthiness to be loved, something which her childhood at Gateshead has not given Jane. When Miss Temple exonerates Jane from Brocklehurst's charges and Jane is received with warmth by the assembled gathering, she feels a 'grievous load' is lifted from her. Freed from the oppression of deprivation for the first time, her mind is released from its preoccupation with survival: 'That night, on going to bed, I forgot to prepare in imagination the Barmecide supper of hot roast potatoes, or white bread and new milk, with which I was wont to amuse my inward cravings: I feasted instead on the spectacle of ideal drawings, which I saw in the dark; all the work of my own hands' (75).

And just as hunger ceases to plague Jane the cold abates correspondingly and she no longer feels herself disabled: 'My wretched feet, flayed and swollen to lameness by the sharp air of January, began to heal and subside under the gentler breathings of April' (76).

At Gateshead Jane has learned that she must fight to survive. At Lowood she discovers that her spiritual health depends as much on reconciliation as on unbridled resistance. Her initial lessons of self-control and moderation come from Helen Burns. It is clear that Jane is, as she herself recognises, 'no Helen Burns' and that she can never totally embrace Helen's doctrine of Christian resignation. Nor should she, the novel seems to suggest, for the logical end to such total self-abnegation is in fact the end that Helen meets in her early death. At the same time, though, Helen does temper Jane's opposite and equally destructive tendency to lash out uncontrollably at every injustice and Jane can at least recognise the challenge of a different perspective: 'Helen Burns considered things by a light invisible to my eyes. I suspected she might be right and I wrong' (56). The first indication of Jane's having internalised something of Helen's 'doctrine of endurance' (56) comes when Jane tells the story of her life at Gateshead to Miss Temple. In contrast to the earlier '[b]itter and truculent' rendition of her woes to Helen (58), Jane resolves to be 'most moderate' in her tale-telling to Miss Temple and she perceives the immediate benefit of her restraint as her story appears 'more credible' and 'fully believed' (72).

A more telling test of Helen's influence comes later in the novel when Jane returns to Gateshead at the request of the dying Mrs Reed. Jane comes to Mrs Reed's deathbed with a 'strong yearning to forget and forgive all injuries' (232) only to feel pain and anger at Mrs Reed's unchanged and unchangeable coldness. At this point Jane's old patterns threaten to reassert themselves, 'My tears had risen, just as in childhood' (233), but now her self-control makes her less vulnerable: 'I ordered them back to their source' (233). As though searching for inspiration Jane recalls Helen Burns, 'listening in thought to her well-remembered tones' (240), before her final confrontation with Mrs Reed. In that meeting it is mature assertion, not childish aggression, that allows Jane to state, 'Love me, then, or hate me, as you will . . . you have my full and free forgiveness: ask now for God's; and be at peace' (242). In this Jane demonstrates that she has become the woman that as a child she felt she must be before she could 'leave' – and leave behind – Gateshead in her life.

The other vital lesson Jane learns from Helen is to temper her craving for love. When Jane declares, '. . . if others don't love me, I would rather die than live . . . to gain some real affection from you, or Miss Temple, or any other whom I truly love, I would willingly submit to have the bone of my arm broken, or to let a bull toss me, or to stand behind a kicking horse, and let it dash its hoof at my chest' (70), the potential for masochism and self-destruction is clear. Such a slavish desire for love represents a particularly dangerous trap for women who are taught to define themselves in terms of their love relationships. Against this attitude in Jane, Helen offers a much-needed challenge: 'Hush, Jane! you think too much of the love of human beings; you are too impulsive, too vehement' (70). Helen's insistence that Jane must look to herself and not to any external authority for her sense of right action – 'If all the world hated you, and believed you wicked, while your own conscience approved you, and absolved you from guilt, you would not be without friends' (70) – might well be a clarion cry for all women labouring under a repressive system of male authority. The relevance of Helen's counselling is evident when Jane faces the prospect of leaving Rochester or staying to become his mistress. Far from her earlier position of love at any cost, Jane sees now that it is better to live without love than to betray herself in getting it. Her resolution of self-respect provides a direct echo of Helen's injunction: '*I* care for myself. The more solitary, the more friendless, the more unsustained I am, the more I will respect myself' (321).

The lesson Jane learns from Helen's endurance is complemented by the example of Miss Temple's moderate action. The headmistress acts as mediator between the patriarchal figure of Brocklehurst and the students at Lowood and in so doing she offers Jane a model for temperate rebellion. As practised by Miss Temple opposition to authority is seen as a viable, respectable form of behaviour, not simply the response of outlaws and children. Miss Temple reinforces Helen's advocacy of truth to self and she provides Jane with a check to her natural recklessness: 'Miss Temple had always something of serenity in her air . . . which precluded deviation into the ardent, the excited, the eager' (73).

However, Miss Temple's serenity provides Jane with a necessary respite – a liberating period of calm in which to learn – rather than an alternative way of living. When Miss Temple departs Jane realises that her mentor and friend has had an anaesthetising effect on her: 'my mind had put off all it had borrowed of Miss Temple – or rather that she had taken with her the serene atmosphere I had been breathing in her vicinity – and that now I was left in my natural element; and beginning to feel the stirring of old emotions' (85).

Jane comes to Thornfield with an excited sense of new possibilities but what emerges is a sense of new threats. From the outset the world of Thornfield is marked by ominous signs of enclosure. As Jane enters its gates they 'clash' behind her, Mrs Fairfax locks the hall door and takes the key before showing Jane to her room, just as she later securely fastens the trapdoor from the attic, and in the library Jane discovers that most of the books are 'locked up behind glass doors' (104). In the face of this enclosure Jane demonstrates a repeated resistance, reminiscent of her gravitation towards the windows in the oppressive space of Gateshead. On her first morning at Thornfield she rises early and leaves the 'vault-like' grandeur of the house to walk outside. In her 'restlessness' she frequently walks in the grounds and approaches the gates to look 'through them along the road' (110). At times her 'sole relief' is to climb to the third storey of the house and survey the distant horizon. It is there that she makes her famous declaration:

> Nobody knows how many rebellions besides political rebellions ferment in the masses of life which people earth. Women are supposd to be very calm generally: but women feel just as men feel; they need exercise for their faculties, and a field for their efforts as much as their brothers do; they suffer from too rigid a restraint, too absolute a stagnation, precisely as men would suffer; and it is narrow-minded in their more privileged fellow-creatures to say that they ought to confine themselves to making puddings and knitting stockings, to playing on the piano and embroidering bags. It is thoughtless to condemn them, or laugh at them, if they seek to do more or learn more than custom has pronounced necessary for their sex.
>
> (111)

The irony of Jane's flight in quest of liberation to the upper-storey of Thornfield is that the third floor is also the site of Bertha Mason's prison. An association is suggested between the two women, most deliberately when Jane's declaration against the 'too rigid . . . restraint of women' is immediately followed with, 'When thus alone, I not unfrequently heard Grace Poole's laugh' (111).

In some ways Bertha can be seen as the antithesis of Jane. She stands as a grim embodiment of passionate extremity – animal-like, uncontrollable, 'intemperate and unchaste' (310). Yet though Jane is no more in danger of embracing Bertha Mason's fate than she was of embracing Helen Burns's, the spectre of Bertha and her madness does seem to lie behind Jane's insistence that she must not surrender to feeling unchecked by conscience:

> I will hold to the principles received by me when I was sane, and not mad – as I am now . . . . They have a worth – so I have always believed; and if I cannot believe it now, it is because I am insane – quite insane: with my veins running fire, and my heart beating faster than I can count its throbs. (322)

At the same time it is possible to recognise Bertha not simply as Jane's opposite – a cautionary contrast – but in some respects as Jane's ally. When Bertha visits Jane's room on the eve of Jane's wedding, it is the prospect of the marriage that she attacks in tearing the veil, not Jane herself. As grotesque as that intervention is, it can nonetheless be compared to the natural omens admonishing Jane against the match. Indeed, Jane rightly interprets the incident 'as a warning of disaster' (280). Repeatedly Jane hears Bertha's laugh when no one else does, as though in special communication. And Jane takes Bertha's part in opposing Rochester's 'vindictive antipathy' towards his wife: 'It is cruel – she cannot help being mad' (305). Rochester's explanation of his marriage to Bertha is most revealing. While condemning Bertha's lack of chastity and temperance, he admits to his own lustful attraction and dissipated wanderings and thus provides Jane with knowledge she needs: 'Mr. Rochester was not to me what he had been; for he was not what I had thought him' (299).

Thornfield offers Jane new opportunities for growth, particularly in the area of her emerging sexuality. The process is hesitant and painful. In the face of her own insecurity, which Rochester deliberately cultivates, Jane is inclined to internalise conventional mores and punish herself by their strictures: 'It does good to no woman to be flattered by her superior, who cannot possibly intend to marry her; and it is madness in all women to let a secret love kindle

within them, which, if unreturned and unknown, must
devour the life that feeds it; and, if discovered and responded
to, must lead, *ignis fatuus*-like, into miry wilds whence there
is no extrication' (163). So, she undertakes the masochistic
exercise of drawing portraits of herself and Blanche for
salutary comparison. This act of self-suppression, seen by
Jane as 'wholesome discipline', is in fact an act of distortion
and self-betrayal. Jane calculatedly chooses the crudest
materials for her own portrait, which she completes in hours,
while she reserves 'smooth ivory' and her finest paints and
brushes for Blanche's portrait which takes many days.

Fortunately, Jane, like her creator, has a strength of ego
that finally will not bow either to false gods or false restraint.
As she later declares in leaving Rochester, she 'cares' about
herself and that fundamental self-respect demands that she
be true to her deepest feelings:

> Do you think, because I am poor, obscure, plain, and
> little, I am soulless and heartless? – You think wrong! – I
> have as much soul as you, – and full as much heart! And if
> God had gifted me with some beauty, and much wealth, I
> should have made it as hard for you to leave me, as it is now
> for me to leave you. I am not talking to you now through
> the medium of custom, conventionalities, nor even of mor-
> tal flesh: – it is my spirit that addresses your spirit; just
> as if both had passed through the grave, and we stood at
> God's feet, equal, – as we are! (256)

Jane's emerging sexuality is paradoxically at once a threat to
self and a means of asserting her ego. This duality is caught in
the consistent use of the imagery of combat in describing
Jane's relationship with Rochester. It is as Jane observes a
'perilous' contest but 'not without its charm' and 'on the
extreme brink' she likes to 'try [her] skill' (306). Jane is
frequently in danger of being overwhelmed by Rochester but
she is also excited by her own power to refuse the submerg-

ence of her identity – 'I crushed his hand, which was ever hunting mine, vigorously, and thrust it back to him red with passionate pressure' (271) – and,her repeated self-assertion represents an important part of her continuing self-definition.

Jane's relationship with Rochester offers her certain kinds of equality. Both she and Rochester stress their 'natural sympath[y]' and mutual kinship. Jane relates to Rochester 'without fear or uneasy restraint' and he acknowledges her as his 'equal' (257), 'good, gifted, lovely' (319). His choice of Jane ahead of Blanche Ingram reverses conventional expectations, exposing as empty the criteria of class and beauty which Jane allowed to rule her comparison of her portrait with Blanche Ingram's.

In short, Rochester's acceptance of Jane seems to offer potent confirmation of her worth. However Jane's extraordinarily negative approach to her wedding day – the month of courtship 'wasted', her 'last hours' 'being numbered', the inability to '[put] off the day' and the prospect that her new identity as Mrs Rochester might be still-born (277) – testifies as much to Jane's mounting unease as to any premonition of Bertha Mason's existence.

Rochester's concept of Jane's equality with him may seem advanced, but it is also dangerously partial. Despite Jane's determination that he should 'know fully' the 'divers rugged points' in her character (276), Rochester consistently depicts Jane as unreal – his 'unearthly thing', 'elfish', 'a fairy', 'witch, sorceress' and 'good genii' – and her power over him as magic. In his self-preoccupied love for Jane he is determined to possess her: 'when once I have fairly seized you, to have and to hold, I'll just – figuratively speaking – attach you to a chain like this' (273). He sees in Jane his 'likeness', not her otherness, and in lavishing jewels and dresses upon her he is responding to his fantasy projection of a lover not to Jane herself: 'the more he bought me, the more my cheek burned with a sense of annoyance and degradation' (271).

Most fundamentally Rochester denies Jane respect and equality by failing to tell her the truth. His deceptions in disguising himself as a gypsy in order to entice Jane to reveal her feelings, in encouraging Jane to think he intends to marry Blanche Ingram and most grievously in failing to tell Jane of Bertha's existence are symptomatic of Rochester's determination to keep control. In a genuinely equal relationship Rochester would accord Jane the opportunity to choose in full knowledge. Instead, his manipulativeness betrays the relationship's ill-health.

On the night before Jane's exodus from Thornfield she dreams of her experience in the red room. Once more she is caught in that childhood prison of passion but now the apparition she merely dreaded as a child does materialise as the moon directs her to 'flee temptation' (324). Throughout the novel Brontë suggests a spiritual link between Jane and a pervasive maternal force embodied in the natural world. In her flight, for example, Jane is aided and nourished by that world: 'Tonight, at least, I would be her guest – as I was her child: my mother would lodge me without money and without price' (328). But as in a maturing mother–daughter relationship, Nature's assistance does not obviate the need for Jane eventually to fend for herself – 'next day, Want came to me, pale and bare'.

Jane's physical ordeal – dispossessed of her belongings, starving and freezing – gives an external reality to her inner emotional desperation. At Moor House she finds a saving warmth and nourishment, although significantly this comes almost exclusively from the female members of the house. Repeatedly the Rivers sisters' warmth is contrasted against the 'freezing spell' of St John. Their simple acceptance of Jane highlights by contrast their brother's suspicious interrogation of her and their concern for her nourishment differs from St John's determination to regulate and restrict her food: 'Now you may eat; though still not immoderately' (350).

Like Brocklehurst, the novel's other religious patriarch, St John fails in every sense to nourish Jane. Even more, he represents a new kind of danger for her. Whereas Rochester has played the role of Edenic tempter, inviting Jane to betray herself in heeding only feeling, St John urges her to follow relentlessly the dictates of reason and deny her passionate nature. Jane in retrospect recognises the destructive polarity of such temptations:

> I was tempted to cease struggling with him – to rush down the torrent of his will into the gulf of his existence, and there lose my own. I was almost as hard beset by him now as I had been once before, in a different way, by another. I was a fool both times. To have yielded then would have been an error of principle; to have yielded now would have been an error of judgment. (423)

Her earlier intellectual recognition that feeling and judgement must be balanced (239) begins to take firm hold as a deep personal conviction when Jane is confronted by the inexorable repressiveness of St John: 'With me' she insists 'it is fully as much a matter of feeling as of conscience' (391).

The crucial test of that conviction comes when the desire for approval and the egotistical thrill at the prospect of complete self-mastery – ' I will show him energies he has not yet seen, resources he has never suspected. Yes: I can work as hard as he can; and with as little grudging' (409) – are checked by the visceral recognition that she cannot betray herself sexually and 'endure all the forms of love': 'such a martyrdom would be monstrous' (410). Jane's final refusal – her no-saying to St John – represents the last necessary affirmation of her own identity and integrity. Her triumph is the achievement of balance in herself, and with her new depth of self-possession she holds her ground against St John: 'It was *my* time to assume ascendancy. *My* powers were in play, and in force. I told him to forebear question or remark; I desired him to leave me: I must, and would be alone. He obeyed at once' (425). No longer in flight as she was from Thornfield, Jane chooses to leave Moor House.

The supernatural prompting of her return to Rochester is more than a matter of literary expediency. Indeed, Brontë takes pain to verify that moment of telepathic communication between the lovers: 'Reader, it was on Monday night – near midnight – that I too had received the mysterious summons: those were the very words by which I replied to it' (453). In doing so, she validates a different kind of knowing – an intuitive, non-rational knowledge which challenges accepted mores. St John and Brocklehurst live in a world of maxims and dogma, drawing justification always from their texts and never from their hearts. Such a world is dangerous for women for it accords them no lawful authority and relegates them to the realm of emotions which it views in turn with suspicion and disdain. Thus, Jane's assertion of only relative power for rationality, 'I am rational *enough*; it is you who misunderstand; or rather, who affect to misunderstand' [my italics] (391) – resonates with particular importance for women.

Critics of *Jane Eyre* have frequently expressed unease about the novel's conclusion, or more specifically about the maimed figure of Rochester in the ending. Clearly the fire at Thornfield is both expedient in getting rid of Bertha and symbolically effective in suggesting some kind of purgation and expiation of the past for Rochester. Yet this does not account for the decision to leave Rochester blind and disfigured. In one sense it seems unnecessary, even gratuitous, since from the first Jane has proved her spiritual and temperamental equality with Rochester, and she returns to him financially autonomous with a fortune of her own. Accordingly, some critics have accused Brontë of a punitive impulse towards her hero, but such a response is too simple. Although the maiming of Rochester represents a fairly crude gesture at equalising power in the relationship, behind it lies Brontë's keen awareness of some disturbing problems for heterosexual equality. Before her return to Marsh End Jane has suffered from Rochester's physical dominance and this inequality has been underscored by Rochester's repeated threats of violence, both figurative and actual. Rochester has always assumed the controlling role 'in a state of proud independence', disdaining 'every part but that of the giver and protector' (451). The physical dependence he experiences as a result of his injuries provides Rochester with the opportunity for new understanding. So, when Jane first comes upon him at Marsh End he is not helpless but nor can he exercise simple control. He is silent and still, perhaps even receptive, in the natural world as he has never been before: 'he seemed to wish by touch to gain an idea of what lay around him: he met but vacancy still; for the trees were some yards off where he stood. He relinquished the endeavour, folded his arms, and stood quiet and mute in the rain, now falling fast on his uncovered head' (437).

Furthermore, this equalising impulse at the end of the novel seems rather less crude and arbitrary when viewed as the last of a sequence of similar impulses which have been employed throughout the novel. The first meeting of Jane and Rochester, for example, sets up the terms of their on-going relationship. Jane is unaware of Rochester's identity as her employer and is thus freed by ignorance from any feeling of economic dependence. Also with Rochester temporarily disabled by his sprained ankle he is in the beginning, as in the end, physically dependent on Jane. And during the course of their relationship the roles are reversed and he is once more dependent on Jane when she saves him from the fire lit by Bertha Mason. Many of the most important encounters between Jane and Rochester take place out of doors – outside the ancestral home, outside the established forms of Rochester's power in a non-social, non-traditional, natural arena. Thus, it is not merely in the ending but repeatedly throughout the novel that Brontë endeavours to envision a heterosexual relationship developing in a context of equal power between women and men.

5 *Shirley*

> If men could see us as we really are, they would be a little
> amazed; but the cleverest, the acutest men are often under
> an illusion about women: they do not read them in a true
> light; they misapprehend them, both for good and evil:
> their good woman is a queer thing, half doll, half angel;
> their bad woman almost always a fiend. (*S* 352)

Shirley represents a significant departure from the style and
concerns of *Jane Eyre* and in many respects this second
published novel lacks the intensity, unity and resolution of
the first. It is transparently schematic, fraught with conflicting impulses and it frequently betrays the effort of composition. Paradoxically, though, the very qualities that might
seem in one sense the least satisfying are in another the things
that make *Shirley* a most intriguing novel and one that sheds a
revealing light on Charlotte Brontë's development as a
woman and a writer.

Brontë's desire for literary success had been long-standing
and deep-rooted. She realised it could be 'a passport to the
society of clever people', a gratifying recognition of her talent
in a world which offered little scope for female achievement
and a means to economic self-sufficiency. And in some
measure it proved to be all this for Charlotte, although her
paralysing shyness made the 'society of clever people' as
much of a trial as a blessing, the recognition she received was
barbed with painful criticism and her financial gains were
only ever relatively modest – indeed, unjustly so. Furthermore, Charlotte could never fully savour the success of
Jane Eyre in a household where her sisters' first novels had
received scant recognition and her brother's relentless de-

cline made it necessary that the very publication of *Jane Eyre* be kept secret from him.

Perhaps the most negative legacy of her sudden success was the anxiety Charlotte felt at the prospect of producing a second novel to rival her first. Her initial impulse was to avoid the task of a new composition by encouraging her publishers to accept a revised version of *The Professor*, the novel they had rejected before *Jane Eyre*. Having failed to convince them and begun *Shirley*, she was anxious 'not to encourage too sanguine an expectation of a favourable reception by the public' (*LL* II 22) and she declared to her publisher, 'far rather would I never publish more than publish anything inferior to my first effort' (*LL* II 307).

This anxiety in Charlotte to reproduce excellence was neither unusual nor especially limited to female writers, although in a nineteenth-century context which did very little to validate female worth, such insecurity was particularly intense for women authors. However the issue of gender does seem pertinent to the new directions undertaken by Brontë in *Shirley* in response to her previous success. In her second novel Charlotte seemed intent on acquiring a 'masculine' authority. *Jane Eyre*, she claimed, had been 'a woman's autobiography, by a woman . . . professedly written' (*LL* III 11). In *Shirley* Brontë abandoned the direct, personal, female voice and opened the novel in a swaggering satiric manner, striving to capture the detachment and knowing sophistication of a third-person narrative voice, 'masculine' by default.

Brontë also created a broad socio-historical perspective for her novel. The 1812 Luddite riots provided a more 'significant' theme than the earlier tale of a solitary governess. Brontë could adopt the role of social commentator and scholar, researching her material in newspapers of the day. Thackeray, whom Brontë deeply admired, was an obvious model and the breadth of his multi-stranded narrative in *Vanity Fair* provides clear parallels with *Shirley*.

Smarting under criticism for the 'coarseness' and 'horrid taste' of *Jane Eyre*, Brontë trod warily in her depiction of sexual passion in *Shirley* and she determined on a story as 'unromantic as Monday morning', having promised the critic George Henry Lewes, 'I will have nothing of what you call "melodramatic"' (*LL* II 179).

In all, then, Brontë's response to the reception of *Jane Eyre* did much to isolate her from the creative wellsprings of her writing. As her first two novels established, *The Professor* negatively and *Jane Eyre* positively, her talent was for the exploration of the individual psyche – especially the female psyche – and the result of working against that in *Shirley* was a rift between the social and personal, between the ostensible Condition-of-England subject and the inner lives of her heroines.

It is possible to argue that the novel has a unifying vision – that in exploring the plight of the female characters and the mill workers it links forms of oppression.[1] However a certain thematic unity is no guarantee of structural unity and the novel remains fragmented at times, wrenching the focus awkwardly between the two heroines, the two heroes and the religious, political and social preoccupations of the work. Brontë herself seemed to perceive the problem in composing the novel when she wrote to her publisher in March 1849: 'how it will be reunited after the long break, or how it can gather force of flow when the current has been checked or rather drawn off so long, I know not' (*LL* II 313). The reason for the 'long break' at this time was the deaths of Branwell and Emily, and Anne's death was yet to come to shatter the flow of Charlotte's work. In later protesting against the comparative undervaluing of *Shirley* Charlotte complained that she had taken 'great pains' with the novel and 'bestowed on it more time, thought and anxiety' than on *Jane Eyre*: 'I did not hurry; I tried to do my best' (*LL* III 154).

In fact, the effort shows: the ideas, schemes and polemic

are never fully integrated. Some of Caroline's and Shirley's most powerful speeches, for example, exist not as dramatic realities in the way of Jane's protests in *Jane Eyre* but much more as 'set pieces', authorial ideas cumbersomely applied. And yet the transparency of Brontë's struggle to write *Shirley* is in itself most revealing. It demonstrates that for all its differences from *Jane Eyre*, *Shirley* is not simply a change in direction but a development of Brontë's thinking on sexual politics. We have seen the twofold nature of Jane Eyre's struggle to negotiate between the extremes of her own character and achieve equality in her sexual relationship. In essence *Shirley*, too, is an attempt at balance but in this novel there is more extended testing of the mythic harmony of *Jane Eyre*. In *Shirley* the dichotomies are not internalised within a single character. Rather the extremes of personality are mediated through the four main characters and the quest for balance and wholeness is not set in the isolated asocial context of Thornfield and Ferndean but in a wider social realm – one which embodies polarities between 'masculine' and 'feminine' spheres.

The early stages of the novel set up not only a simple disjunction but a positive antagonism between an industry-centred male world and a nature-centred female world. One feature of the opening scenes between the three curates, for example, is that their male camaraderie is marked by their thoughtless contempt for their landladies. In their round of visits, which the landladies see as a 'system of mutual invasion', female presence is only tolerated so that the men may be served.

When Malone leaves Donne's lodgings and walks to Robert Moore's mill, he enters another distinctively male world. The 'huge black mill' with all it represents of commerce and power stands in stark contrast to the 'little white house' at the opposite end of the property where Moore's sister Hortense fashions an unswervingly domestic sphere: 'a snug nest for content and contemplation, but one within which the wings of action and ambition could not long lie folded'.[2] Moore's mill is a jealously guarded domain. Robert maintains a deliberate policy of exclusion with his determination 'to have every convenience within myself, and not to be dependent on the feminity in the cottage yonder for every mouthful I eat or every drop I drink' (26) – Malone heartily encourages this safeguard against 'petticoat government' as 'proper order' and he and Moore vie with each other to establish their misogynistic credentials. So, Malone declares 'the ladies are best alone. I never was a lady's man' (22) and Moore affirms 'I seek female society about as assiduously as you do, Mr. Malone' (23). Appropriately, Moore is attended in this world by his foreman Joe Scott, the novel's coarsest misogynist.

All the males, ruling and ruled alike, derive pleasure from the prospect of violence. Malone has come to the mill feeling 'never . . . more in tune for a shindy' (18). Moore keeps watch for the arrival of his new machinery with 'a sense of war-like excitement' and despite the fact that his frames are ruined, the prospect of a vengeful fight enlivens him with a 'new-found vivacity' and rouses him to 'the best possible spirits' (36). The frame-breakers on their side 'would have had great pleasure in shooting either of the leaders from behind a wall' (36).

Both heroines make explicit protest against this prevailing 'war-like' spirit. Caroline chastises Moore for the harshness of his attitude towards the workers: 'I cannot help thinking it unjust to include all poor working people under the general and insulting name of "the mob," and continually to think of them and treat them haughtily' (93). Similarly, before the riot Shirley attempts to use her financial power to defuse the mounting tension between employer and employee and having failed to do so, she pointedly refers to the injured rioters as Moore's 'victims'.

The repeated distinction between masculine and feminine spheres is never more clear than on the occasion of the riot itself. The male participants have attempted to remove all women not only from the vicinity but from knowledge of the action. Thus Hortense has been despatched to stay at Miss Mann's and Shirley has been deputised as 'honorary male' to guard over Caroline at the Rectory. When Caroline and Shirley make their way to the scene, nonetheless, to bring warning to Robert, Brontë is at pains to stress their separateness from the violence. While the attack takes place within their sight, they stand at a vantage point removed from the scene as Shirley observes, 'alone with the friendly night, its mute stars, and these whispering trees, whose report our friends will not come to gather' (343).

Shirley's description draws attention to the association of the females with the peaceful natural world which is contrasted against the males' imperviousness to it. Indeed, a similar point has been made earlier in the description of Malone's walk to the mill. As he strides 'doggedly' towards his destination in the hope of a fight, he is oblivious to the rain clouds above: 'Malone was not a man given to close observation of Nature; her changes passed, for the most part, unnoticed by him: he could walk miles on the most varying April day, and never see the beautiful dallying of earth and heaven' (19). Later Shirley refuses to heed the bells 'summoning all to the church' where she must hear a succession of male speeches: 'I will stay out here with my mother Eve, in these days called Nature' (321).

In the scene that follows Shirley discourses on her vision of Eve, 'a woman-Titan' and not the 'cook' of Milton's version. In communion with 'the warm summer evening' Shirley falls into 'a pleasurable trance' (321). Her experience is no less spiritual than the proceedings within the church but it is alien to the established modes of Shirley's society in which the male hegemony is markedly unreceptive to any non-rational influence. Robert Moore, for example, urges Caroline to judge with her head and not her heart and Mr Helstone likewise refuses to acknowledge any dominion for feeling:

'When women are sensible – and, above all, intelligible – I can get on with them. It is only the vague, superfine sensations, and extremely wire-drawn notions, that put me about. Let a woman ask me to give her an edible or a wearable . . . I can, at least understand the demand: but when they pine for they know not what – sympathy – sentiment – some of these indefinite abstractions – I can't do it: I don't know it; I haven't got it'. (440)

The polarity between worlds is further stressed by the way in which the male antagonism towards the female is matched by an answering female exclusiveness, seen particularly in the repeated female fantasies about escape to an all-female world. When Shirley plans to take Caroline on a picnic, for example, to the aptly named Nunnwood forest, she insists that she and Caroline go alone: 'the presence of gentlemen' dispels quietude and causes the women to 'forget Nature' (214). Similarly, Shirley proposes to take Caroline on holiday to the Scottish Highlands where she will play the role of Captain Keeldar and Caroline will be her genial comrade. Mrs Pryor, too, plans to take Caroline away to 'a house of my own' and her intentions mirror Caroline's earlier wish that her mother would appear and say, 'Caroline, my child, I have a home for you; you shall live with me' (322).

Having set up these overt oppositions, the novel then proceeds to undermine them. This simple antagonism and division between spheres is gradually revealed to be both artificial and harmful. The opposing spheres are the constructions of a society working with false dichotomies, creating characters who while functioning within conventional sex roles are actually denying a part of themselves.

Each of the four major characters is trapped in some ways by the roles they adopt. The fantasised separatist self-sufficiency of each character – Robert at his mill, Louis in his projected North American journey, Shirley and Caroline in their planned Scottish expeditions – depends on the concealment and denial of true feelings. Each character lives a lie, loving where they dare not show and repressing their emotions in a crippling manner. Accordingly each breaks down, stricken by illness.

The stress of such self-repression and denial is seen clearly in the character of Robert Moore. For all the harshness of his public face, he harbours a gentler, more sensitive side: 'But I find in myself, Lina, two natures; one for the world and business, and one for home and leisure. Gérard Moore is a hard dog, brought up to mill and market: the person you call your cousin Robert is sometimes a dreamer, who lives elsewhere than in Cloth-hall and counting-house' (256). The tension between these two aspects of his personality is repeatedly dramatised. In his personal life Robert is naturally drawn towards things which would associate him with the 'feminine' sphere of the novel. He is a gentle and gifted teacher, unlocking problems for Caroline which Hortense cannot elucidate, and he is equally benign in his treatment of the Yorke children. Despite his adversary relationship with the natural world in his position as mill-owner, Robert's responsiveness to nature is evident in his long night walks and his cultivation of the cottage garden. His enthusiasm in the Shakespeare reading demonstrates that the imaginative world has a similar charm. Above all he is attracted to Caroline who is in many ways the 'feminine' centre of the novel.

However Robert is unable to accept this side of his personality and is ruthless in his repression of it. He condemns his feeling for Caroline as 'weakness' and 'frenzy', for example, and he compensates for his lapses into softness by assuming his 'masculine' role once more with redoubled vigour: 'by the next morning he was sure to be frozen up again' (78). Living in such bad faith, Robert ultimately allows himself to betray his integrity by the mercenary offer of marriage to Shirley.

In many respects Shirley might seem the character least

trapped by conventional sex roles. She is enormously liberated by her position as a landowner and heiress and she enjoys a standing and power within the community that Caroline can only envy. However it is not as a woman – not as herself – that Shirley's strength is recognised. In almost every way Shirley must adopt the guise of the 'masculine' world, escaping one role only to be bound by another, in order to act as an effective social agent. That imposition is clear even in the most personal detail of her name: 'They gave me a man's name; I hold a man's position: it is enough to inspire me with a touch of manhood' (200). She speaks of herself, and is spoken of, as a male, Captain Keeldar, and more tellingly her dialogue betrays a habit of speaking of herself in the third person which underlines the split which is forced upon her: 'why I began to flatter myself we were thoroughly friends; that you liked Shirley almost as well as Shirley likes you: and she does not stint her regard' (242). Shirley is not simply admired as a strong woman, she is tolerated as an exceptional one. In so far as she is deemed an 'honorary male', her gifts are appropriated by the masculine sphere. This is most evident on the night of the riot when Helstone asks her to guard his house and sees himself as bestowing on her a temporary male power. So, in reluctantly giving her the pistols, he declares, 'It is paying you a great compliment, captain, to lend you these' (334). Just how temporary and fundamentally insignificant that investiture is Shirley herself recognises: 'They won't trust me . . . that is always the way when it comes to the point' (314).

Ironically, then, Shirley is no less trapped in role-playing than Robert, and the betrayal of self is for Shirley even more fundamental given the transsexual nature of her public persona. As Captain Keeldar Shirley is committed to public masquerades and personal silence. Thus she finally complains to Louis: 'I am neither so strong, nor have I such pride in my strength, as people think' (513). The harmfulness of the constraint which shapes Shirley's behaviour is emphasised by the way in which her secretiveness about the dog bite threatens both her health and peace of mind.

While Caroline and Louis are also oppressed by their assigned roles, their suffering lies in the reverse of Robert's and Shirley's. Where Robert and Shirley feel divorced from their gentler emotional selves, Caroline and Louis find themselves restricted to this realm without any other outlet. Those nineteenth-century readers who stressed Caroline's 'feminine' appeal failed to recognise that her demure 'femininity' is in large measure the product of her repression. Her childhood experience with a dissolute father, 'shut up, day and night, in a high garret-room' (103) and frequently left without food, foreshadows an adult life of enclosure and denial with her misogynist uncle. Caroline is 'too still' and 'nearly smothered' in her life at the Rectory and she wonders restively if she is 'always to be curbed and kept down?' (347). The yearning in Caroline for a different lot is painfully clear: she longs for an occupation or profession 'fifty times a day' (229) and her potential for a more active and meaningful existence is repeatedly suggested. She demonstrates 'a spirit no one could have expected of her' (91) in her reading of Shakespeare and in her daring confrontation with Mrs Yorke. Significantly, it is Shirley more than anyone who recognises Caroline's strengths, perceiving that despite Caroline's quiet demeanour 'there is both a force and a depth somewhere within' (263) and acknowledging that Caroline has 'twice – ten times my strength of mind on certain subjects' (266). Yet that potential is consistently denied as Caroline is forced to play out her mindless role as Helstone's niece – 'put all crochets out of your head and run away and amuse yourself' (191) – with the result that her unchannelled energy becomes self-consuming.

Given her fate, it is not surprising that Caroline in turn should be sensitive to Louis's powerlessness, recognising how much he is regarded as 'a mere teacher' and how little as 'a gentleman', or more pertinently 'a man'. Louis like

Caroline is 'still' and 'grave' and he lives a life of constriction, his 'faculties . . . walled up in him' (455). His role as a tutor within the Sympson family gives no scope to the depth of his emotional and imaginative impulses. When he advises Harry that his mind is a 'captive' lying in 'physical bondage' and that he will find 'natural release' (465) for his soul in writing, Louis might well be diagnosing his own condition. He himself finds release in his diary and he tolerates 'confinement to a small, still corner of the real world very patiently' because he nourishes 'a large world of his own in his own head and heart' (519). The danger and unsatisfactoriness of such an internalised life, denied of expression, is that it can become, like Caroline's, self-consuming. So, appropriately, when Louis becomes ill, he suffers – like Caroline – from fever.

These tensions within the characters reveal that any exclusively 'masculine' or 'feminine' world rests on a denial of wholeness. It is significant that Brontë treats these qualities not as inherent gender-determined characteristics but as cultural constructs. Sensitivity and imaginativeness, for all they are generally regarded as 'feminine', are no more exclusively female qualities than strength and bravery are male. The health, both physical and psychic, of each character depends on their recognition of their suppressed selves. Robert, for example, learns what it is to be denied power in a sexual relationship when he is refused by Shirley and through his experience of powerlessness in sexual humiliation, financial ruin and illness he confronts his earlier limitations: 'Unless I am more considerate to ignorance, more forbearing to suffering than I have hitherto been, I shall scorn myself as grossly unjust' (543). Similarly, Shirley admits her vulnerability in her confession to Louis of her fear of rabies, Caroline forsakes her passivity in her decisive action in going to Robert in his illness and Louis sheds the subservience of economic dependence in asserting his love for Shirley. All, then, have in some sense moved towards that personal ideal of balance and wholeness which, as we have seen, was so important in the resolution of *Jane Eyre*.

In *Shirley* this balancing is built into the very structure of the novel. Initially the four major characters occupy extreme positions of 'masculine' and 'feminine' male and 'masculine' and 'feminine' female. The balancing is begun by each character's acknowledgement of their 'other' side and completed in the 'cross-matching' that occurs in the pairing of males and females – Robert with Caroline, Shirley with Louis. In a sense each is reconciled with the 'other' in themselves in an androgynous ideal.

It is a calculatedly neat conclusion and yet despite this, it fails to satisfy. Instead, the closing chapters betray more sense of disturbance and discontent than of resolution. The concluding paragraphs, for example, read like a lament for the destruction of the natural world, not a celebration of the success of Robert's industrial world. The Hollow which was 'once green, and lone, and wild', 'a bonnie spot – full of oak trees and nut trees' is now a scene of 'stone and brick and ashes' with its 'cinder-black highway' and workman's cottages. The reported disappearance of the 'fairy' inhabitants of the Hollow suggests the demise of an imaginative realm and of a capacity to see the world in something beyond man-centred terms.

The second focus for unease in the novel's conclusion lies in the character of Shirley. Her deep reluctance to face her marriage to Louis undermines the conventional happiness of the double wedding. When Louis complains of Shirley's aloof refusal to fix a date for their wedding and his 'present uncertain unsettled state', Shirley's reply – 'you don't know how happy you are! – any change will be for the worse!' (631) – sounds ominous, especially at the end of a novel which has presented a gallery of failed and unhappy marriages. Images of confinement and restriction confirm the sense that Shirley is somehow reduced in her relationship with Louis:

It had needed a sort of tempest-shock to bring her to the point; but there she was at last, fettered to a fixed day: there she lay, conquered by love, and bound with a vow.

Thus vanquished and restricted, she pined, like any other chained denizen of deserts. Her captor alone could cheer her; his society only could make amends for the lost privilege of liberty: in his absence, she sat or wandered alone; spoke little, and ate less. (638)

Perhaps a sense of disappointment at Shirley's fate stems from the fact that she has been Brontë's most independent and outspoken heroine and therefore it seems she has most to lose in compromise. Brontë herself seems unable to reconcile the notion of a heroine with strength, independence and integrity and the idea of that heroine's involvement in an engrossing sexual relationship. The effort to achieve a balance between independence and dependence is clear in almost every exchange between Louis and Shirley in the concluding chapters. So, Shirley is at once Louis's 'pupil' and his 'sovereign'; Louis is the 'keeper' of the 'tamed' lioness but Shirley is a 'wily, tameless' pantheress and leopard; in the classroom Shirley's imaginative power is balanced by her imitative bent; Louis is Shirley's 'master' and she is his 'idol'; Louis attains the power of Fieldhead only as Shirley 'abdicates'. Shirley's desire for mutuality, seen in the wish that Louis '*share* the burden' and be master '*where* I am faulty' [my italics], is obscured by a lingering wish to be dominated – one at odds with her sense of suffocation at the prospect of 'never be[ing] my own mistress more. A terrible thought!' (216). In a way reminiscent of *The Professor* the overall effect is not so much of a sense of balance as of uneasy veering.

More broadly, the novel leaves too many questions unanswered. Its achievement lies in the problems it recognises, and its disappointment in its failure to come to terms with those problems. The novel has offered, for example, an

extended study through a variety of relationships of the lack
of understanding between the sexes:

> If men could see us as we really are, they would be a little
> amazed; but the cleverest, the acutest men are often under
> an illusion about women: they do not read them in a true
> light; they misapprehend them, both for good and evil:
> their good woman is a queer thing, half doll, half angel;
> their bad woman almost always a fiend. (352)

It demonstrates, too, how that lack of understanding can be
compounded into antagonism and dislike in a figure like Mr
Helstone who 'neither respected nor liked the sex' (115). The
jaundiced accounts of Helstone, Mrs Pryor and Mrs Yorke
of the miseries of married life are matched by the brutal
imagery with which Brontë comtemplates a loveless match:

> . . . her parents, I say, would have delivered Hannah over
> to his lovingkindness and his tender mercies without one
> scruple; and the second Mrs. Helstone, inversing the
> natural order of insect existence, would have fluttered
> through the honeymoon a bright, admired butterfly, and
> crawled the rest of her days a sordid, trampled worm. (117)

Despite this bleak outlook any woman who seeks independence faces an equally forbidding prospect as Caroline's plight
demonstrates. Her desire for occupation is ignored by her
cousin and dismissed by her uncle, and her only models for
socially-sanctioned female independence involve either distortion or annihilation of the ego, seen respectively in
Shirley's 'masculine' role-playing and Miss Mann's and Miss
Ainley's selfless charity. It is not surprising, then, that
Caroline sees her alternatives as 'dropping off in comsump-
tion or decline; or, what is worse, degenerating to sour old
maids, – envious, backbiting, wretched, because life is a
desert to them; or, what is worst of all, reduced to strive, by

scarce modest coquetry and debasing artifice, to gain that position and consideration by marriage, which to celibacy is denied' (392).

As a consequence of such enforced social and sexual passivity women are in danger of destroying themselves. In a society where it is the 'best wisdom' to 'ask no questions; utter no remonstrances' – to take the scorpion fate has offered in one's palm, 'close your fingers firmly upon the gift' and 'let it sting your palm' (105) – repression and masochism must be the norm for women.

In the face of this clear-sightedness, then, the resolution of the novel's ending seems artificial. Brontë perceives the social evils but stops short of pursuing the social change. She relies for her sense of resolution on the power of personal change. In the asocial setting of Ferndean this seems a more convincing option, but in the socially anchored world of *Shirley* the solution seems more like an evasion. At the end of the novel it is the circumstances not the system which have changed. Happy marriage is no more a fundamental answer for women's oppression than improved economic conditions are for workers' oppression. Each ameliorates the symptoms but leaves the root causes untouched. For all her willingness to perform a comedy-like sleight of hand at the end of the novel, Brontë seems aware that there is still cause for protest. The sombre uneasiness of the conclusion reads like a tacit recognition of the inadequacy of the novel's compromises.

6 Villette

> So this subject is done with. It is right to look our
> life-accounts bravely in the face now and then, and settle
> them honestly. (451)

After the publication of *Shirley* Charlotte Brontë tried yet
again to resurrect *The Professor* rather than begin a new
novel. Once more her publishers refused the work and
Brontë resolved to consign this early book, now wryly
deemed her 'idiot child', to a 'cupboard by himself'
(*LL* III 206–7). In truth, however, she did not completely
relinquish *The Professor* but set about reworking the basic
material which she transformed into her final novel *Villette*.

The two novels provide revealing contrasts not simply in
terms of craft – the raw talent of her early work against the
sure accomplishment of her later art – but in terms of vision.
Perhaps the most obvious reworking from the earlier to the
later work is the change from a male narrator in *The Professor*
to a female narrator in *Villette*. As we might expect, this
change facilitated a more authentic, less strained narrative
voice for, as Brontë herself admitted, 'When I write about
women I am sure of my ground – in the other case, I am not so
sure' (*LL* II 312). More importantly, though, the change in
narrator was enormously liberating for Brontë imaginatively,
enabling the exploration of female powerlessness and repression at a deeper level than she had ever touched upon before.
In *Villette* the narrator's vulnerability is repeatedly linked to
her gender, as a contrast with *The Professor* makes clear.
Lucy Snowe is cheated on several occasions because she is
easily taken advantage of as a woman. She has no entrée into
this Continental world and wanders the streets of Villette lost

and pursued by threatening men in marked contrast to Crimsworth who can count on patronage to make his way clear when he arrives with Hunsden's letter of introduction. Symptomatically, Lucy, unlike Crimsworth, is uneasy with her money (and all that that implies of social power), unaware of the ways of this world and unable either literally or figuratively to speak its language. Where Lucy is repeatedly trapped and enclosed, Crimsworth finds release in long walks in the fresh air. Further, Lucy is condemned by virtue of her sex to adopt a passive role sexually whereas Crimsworth can take the initiative in his relationships, rebuffing Zoraïde Reuter and seeking out Frances.

These local contrasts point to the more general difference of Brontë's last novel. *Villette* is at once more unflinching in its content and more sophisticated in its style than any of her earlier works, reflecting Brontë's maturity both as a woman and a writer. Lucy Snowe, like her predecessors, still craves for love, but in exploring her heroine's quest on this occasion Brontë forswears the elements of idealism and romance evident in *Jane Eyre* and portrays Lucy as much more convincingly 'plain' than Jane Eyre. Neurotic, cold, passive and unreliable, Lucy lives up to Brontë's intention that her heroine 'should not occupy the pedestal to which "Jane Eyre" was raised by some injudicious admirers. She is where I meant her to be, and where no charge of self-laudation can touch her' (*LL* IV 52). Similarly, Brontë resists in *Villette* the compromises and evasions that persist uneasily in *Shirley*.

In her last work Brontë seems intent on facing the harshest realities for, as her heroine observes, 'To see and know the worst is to take from Fear her main advantage'.[1] Things that existed as passing spectres in the earlier novels – loneliness, loss, sexual threat – are relentless facts, deeply felt in *Villette*.

Villette has been seen as a return to the successes of *Jane Eyre* after failure in the experiment with the socio-historical novel in *Shirley*. Certainly in its first-person narrative and its preoccupation with the individual psyche *Villette* does draw on the strengths developed in *Jane Eyre*. However, the similarity should not obscure the important differences. In contrast to Jane Eyre's direct, accurate and trustworthy narrative Lucy Snowe's story-telling is frequently vague, distorted and unreliable. In this new development Brontë makes complex use not simply of the story of Lucy's life but of the quality of Lucy's narrative itself to explore the neuroses of her heroine.

Furthermore, although both novels concentrate on the single subject, the nature of that focus on the individual has changed. In *Jane Eyre* the heroine assumes complete central-ity and other characters exist primarily in so far as they interact with Jane. Accordingly, the novel's resolutions take place in an asocial world with Jane and Rochester living in seclusion at Ferndean. In *Villette*, however, the focus on the single subject is accompanied by a disturbing recognition of the effects that social repression have on the individual. Even in *Shirley*, which is ostensibly much more concerned with the problems of the individual living in society, the effects of social repression are seen as transitory. For all Caroline's and Shirley's sufferings both women emerge relatively unscathed once their lot has been alleviated by fortuitous circumstance. In *Villette* Brontë explores the indelible imprint of repression on the individual – the deeply internalised scarring that makes Lucy Snowe the difficult woman that she is.

The novel opens with the first of Lucy's evasions – her focus on the young Paulina. What might initially seem like a puzzling distraction is in fact a characteristic manoeuvre on Lucy's part to avoid attention by remaining on the periphery and to escape suffering by living vicariously through the lives of others.

Paulina's story serves a further purpose, presenting in the details of her childhood a typical example of the kinds of socialisation to which females are subjected. Paulina is appropriately pretty, fastidiously neat and 'happy' when surrounded by her sewing and dolls. In her miniature form she exemplifies the 'perfect' wife and mother, adopting both roles in turn for her father and Graham Bretton. Paulina seeks out service to males as her *raison d'être*, anxiously providing for the food and comfort of her menfolk. The disturbingly masochistic dimension of that service is illustrated in the incident where Paulina hems a handkerchief for her father: '. . . pricking herself ever and anon, marking the cambric with a track of minute red dots; occasionally starting when the perverse weapon – swerving from her control – inflicted a deeper stab than usual; but still silent, diligent, absorbed, *womanly*' [my italics] (73), and again when she lies at Graham's feet and caresses 'the heedless foot' that has just kicked her.

Paulina's animation depends on her role-playing with Graham: 'In his absence she was a still personage' (82). After being rebuffed from the male world of Graham's party, Paulina learns a lesson in 'womanly' passivity. She never again makes the mistake of intruding, or making demands, or showing desire. Instead, she resolves always to 'wait'. In her hymn recital, as in all else, Paulina learns to perform in the approved manner, proving in her lessons with Graham to be 'apt in imitating' (86). In all, her ego is subsumed in the male she serves: 'her pleasure was to please Graham' (86).

Paulina 'successfully' moulds herself, then, in the way her world requires and she is rewarded in the end with marriage to the socially desirable and eminently suitable Dr John. Lucy is no less shaped – and scarred – by her world, although in Lucy the consequences are manifest in ways that are more simply regarded as negative. In many respects Lucy Snowe is the true daughter of a society in which repression and disguise are necessary strategies for women striving to behave appropriately and all the less attractive features of her personality, which Brontë characterises as 'morbid and weak', can be seen as direct reflections of social pressures.

In various forms, for example, Lucy is deceptive and unreliable, and this is reflected directly in her narration.

Most simply, she withholds information, omitting to inform
the reader of her recognition of Dr John's true identity or
deliberately suppressing the name of the person who presents
her with the cherished white violets. Similarly, Lucy is
deliberately vague, as with the details of her life after
Bretton. She is inclined to draw attention to her own
unreliability, almost as though taunting the reader and
cancelling any tacit contract of credibility. After describing
her dreams of Europe, for example, she declares abruptly:
'Cancel the whole of that, if you please, reader – or rather let
it stand' (118) and later when she resolves 'to speak truth,
and drop that tone of false calm' (350), she casts doubt by
implication on the accuracy of all that has gone before. That
suspicion is substantiated by the frequent discrepancy
between the state Lucy declares and the language with which
she describes it. So, in the same sentence as Lucy pleads
'guiltless of that curse, an overheated and discursive imagination', she admits that the sight of Paulina alone with, as
Lucy floridly describes, 'her head in her pigmy hand', leaves
Lucy inclined to believe the room 'not inhabited, but
haunted' (69).

It is important to recognise, however, that Lucy's deception and unreliability are the means by which she constructs a
self-protective façade – and façades are precisely what Lucy's
society encourages in females. Women exist two-
dimensionally, defined by the externals of appearance and
connections. It is no accident that Lucy is preoccupied by her
reflection in the mirror, for in her world that superficial
image is taken to be the sum of Lucy's self. Her third
dimension – her inner life – is denied and disregarded by all
except Paul, and Lucy lives in danger of the ultimate
victimisation – of regarding herself only 'as others see me'
and inhabiting, chameleon-like, the character others create
for her:

Madame Beck esteemed me learned and blue; Miss

Fanshawe, caustic, ironic, and cynical; Mr. Home, a model teacher, the essence of the sedate and discreet: somewhat conventional perhaps, too strict, limited and scrupulous, but still the pink and pattern of gover-ness-correctness; whilst another person, Professor Paul Emanuel, to wit, never lost an opportunity of intimating his opinion that mine was rather a fiery and rash nature – adventurous, indocile, and audacious. (386)

In this world of surface Lucy has little claim. She is 'nobody's daughter' whom 'nobody minded', effaced to the point of seeing herself as a 'shadow' and condemned to a 'haunting dread of . . . outward deficiency' (583).

The split in Lucy, then, between her deceptive façade and her inner self is no mere foible or individual shortcoming, her own neurotic construction. It is, rather, an understandable response to a world which deals in mirror images – or equally two-dimensional painted images – of women. In fact, Brontë understood personally how social dictates could force such a split upon one. In a letter describing the difficulty of fulfilling the accepted role of a governess she lamented the 'estrangement from one's real character – the adoption of a cold frigid apathetic exterior that is painful' (*LL* I 241).

There is a further dimension to Lucy's deceptive façade, as she herself explains: 'There is a perverse mood of the mind which is rather soothed than irritated by misconstruction; and in quarters where we can never be rightly known, we take pleasure, I think, in being consummately ignored' (164). In aiding that 'misconstruction' at times, Lucy confounds others by refusing to dispense knowledge of herself either to the reader or to the characters with whom she interacts. She thus reserves for herself the power of the liar in that degree of control that comes from operating with knowledge that others are denied. It is only a minimal sphere of control and in many ways a self-defeating strategy, but it is one option for the powerless struggling for survival.

Lucy's passivity and coldness are also disturbing features of her personality but they, too, can be seen as a reflection – or perhaps a distortion – of 'appropriate' womanly behaviour. Paulina, the exemplar of 'femininity', knows better than to reveal her feelings in a betrayal of love for Graham. Accordingly, in response to Graham's initiative in writing to her Paulina replies trembling 'for fear of making the answer too cordial' (466). She writes three versions of a letter, gradually censoring and repressing her feelings, 'chastening and subduing the phrases at every rescript', until she produces the 'morsel of ice' (466) she knows will meet Graham's approval. Whereas Villette society tolerates and even indulges the emotional outbursts and 'histrionic lessons' of Paul Emanuel, passion in women is regarded as unacceptable, the recourse of outlaws like the actress Vashti.

In some respects Lucy's passivity in the face of Mme Beck's spying and intrusions seems bewildering and infuriating. On her first night at Rue Fossette, for example, Lucy feigns sleep while she watches Mme Beck inspect 'every article' of her clothing, purse and memorandum-book. This gross invasion of privacy is accompanied by what seems almost a violation of her person as Mme Beck carries her examination to the extreme of approaching Lucy's apparently sleeping figure and 'gazing at my face. She then drew nearer, bent close over me; slightly raised my cap, and turned back the border so as to expose my hair' (131). Despite this, Lucy concludes sedately that although Mme Beck's behaviour was 'very un-English', its 'end was not bad'. She continues to respond in a similar way throughout much of the novel, admiring the 'adroitness' with which Mme Beck conducts her searches and waiting 'peaceably' for the return of her stolen letters (377). This acquiescence seems to betray the mentality of a classic victim but it is understandable, nonetheless, for as the novel makes clear, her acceptance and success at Rue Fossette depend upon it. It is no more than is expected of her from the system in which she must survive.

From an early age Lucy has internalised the lesson that the female who initiates action is liable to be hurt. So, she perceives the young Paulina's untutored action in spontaneously embracing Graham as 'strangely rash' and her response reveals her own deep apprehension: Paulina's action excited 'the feeling one might experience on seeing an animal dangerous by nature, and but half-tamed by art, too heedlessly fondled' (87). Lucy herself must be 'goaded, driven, stung, forced' into action and she reveals that she is not merely 'tame and still by habit' but 'disciplined by destiny' (97). That discipline or conditioning has so permeated Lucy that it has shaped her way of seeing the world. She lives her life braced against the future and continually casting herself as the victim of insuperable forces – 'Fate', 'Providence', 'Destiny'. She adopts, in short, 'the language of passivity'.[2]

Deception, coldness and passivity, then, provide Lucy Snowe with a means of survival. However, they constitute adopted strategies, not simply inherent character traits. The distinction is evident in the effort Lucy needs to make to maintain her façade. She admits, for example, that it was 'seldom I could properly act out my resolution to be reserved and cool where I had been grieved and hurt' (406). After any lapse Lucy steadfastly resumes her persona: 'the next day I was again Lucy Snowe' (187), and she maintains it with painful and systematic self-suppression: 'I studiously held the quick of my nature' (175). Seen in this light Lucy's deficiencies are more an indictment of the system which has produced her than a measure of her personal worth. Much of the power and interest of Brontë's characterisation of Lucy Snowe lies in the awareness of the potential in the heroine which exceeds her customary role-playing and the tension that exists between Lucy's 'two lives – the life of thought, and that of reality' (140).

The focus on Lucy's negative qualities is largely due to Lucy herself. Her inclination to present herself in the least flattering light tends to obscure the fact that Lucy has the potential and desire to rise above her chill, passive persona. She sporadically protests that she 'still felt life' (96) and 'had feelings' (175) and she is herself 'mutinous' against her own repressive strategies. She demonstrates a yearning for something beyond her circumscribed existence and 'always-fettered wings' (108) that militates against her tendency towards passive acquiescence. At decisive moments she musters genuine courage, as when she decides in London that 'it was better to go forward than backward, and that I *could* go forward' (107). Similarly, despite a characteristic description of her 'usual base habit of cowardice' Lucy accepts the 'challenge of strength' Mme Beck offers in requesting that Lucy teach at Rue Fossette. Mme Beck, indeed, echoes Lucy's former resolution when she demands 'Will you . . . go backward or forward?' (141). This pattern is repeated in Lucy's decision to act in the play. Despite her diffidence and her acceptance of the part to please M. Paul, Lucy again rises to the challenge and ultimately acts with 'power', 'to please [her]self' (211). Although Lucy's ambition finds little scope for expression in her repressed character, Lucy concedes that she is 'a good deal bent on success' and feels pleasure at 'getting on; not lying the stagnant prey of mould and rust' (145).

At times, too, Lucy demonstrates a revealing independence of spirit. At the gallery, for example, she is happy in 'examining, questioning, and forming conclusions' about the art works and despite Paul's bullying, she refuses to be impressed by the conventional representations of women in the serial painting 'La vie d'une femme', which she finds 'flat, dead, pale and formal' (277). And she displays no more respect for convention in her comic refusal at the opera to swap her prize of a cigar-case with Graham's of 'a lady's head-dress' (300).

Lucy's public persona, then, is an effacement and a betrayal of her fullest self. In her need to develop beyond this

divided self Lucy resembles all of Brontë's heroines in their
growth towards psychic health. And as with her predecessors,
a shaping force in Lucy's growth is her developing relationship with the hero, M. Paul. When Paul demands to
know from his student actresses if their flesh has turned to
snow and their blood to ice and urges them to put fire into
their performance, he foreshadows the role he is to play in
Lucy's life. Repeatedly seen as 'fiery' and able to melt the
'snow-statues' of the classroom with his 'intemperate heat',
Paul can dissolve the icy façade of Lucy Snowe. He
recognises Lucy's passionate nature from the start and he
consistently holds up to her a vision of the self she represses,
thus acting as a truer 'mirror' than the glittering glass at the
opera. By repeated provocation he challenges Lucy to give
expression to her suppressed feelings and his own demonstrative nature validates a mode of behaviour that Lucy has
previously shunned.

In receiving love, Lucy learns to love herself. Indeed, in
one sense loving Paul is a gesture of self-love in so far as he
represents those qualities in herself that she has refused to
value. Her infatuation wth Graham, on the other hand,
threatens to reinforce all her defensive strategies and self-
division. Graham scorns the open display of feeling especially
in women, as his 'branding judgement' of Vashti and his
admiration of Mme Beck's self-control illustrate. His chill
manner, 'constitutionally suave and serene' (296) provides
marked contrast against the warmth of Paul's enthusiasm
and 'over-eagerness'. Graham is blind to Lucy's passionate
nature and to her sexual identity. Graham dismisses Lucy's
sense of reality by ascribing her vision of the nun to her
neurosis, whereas Paul confirms Lucy's vision.

Lucy feels a particular 'affinity' and 'rapport' with Paul.
Each lives a deprived and enclosed life in the service of
others, although they share a passionate nature. Both have
'buried' their feelings as Paul acknowledges when he concedes that the ghostly nun – the spectre of a repressed self –

has as much business with him as with Lucy (457). Thus in her choice of male Lucy must choose for or against herself and her allegiance to Paul forms an act of self-validation.

Lucy's love of Paul forces her to acknowledge the strength of her feeling. On the night of the fête, for example, when she sees Paul with Marie, Lucy feels jealousy as she has never felt 'till now': 'a vulture so strong in beak and talon' (567). The strength of the feeling compels Lucy into an unequivocal admission to herself of her emotions. She returns to the school and sees the nun once more, but significantly on this occasion Lucy is 'not overcome' and 'lashed up by a new scourge, I defied spectra' (569). She confronts the 'old phantom' and destroys it, thereby figuratively putting to death that embodiment of repressive forces.

Whereas Lucy has consistently seen emotion as a source of vulnerability, she now begins to recognise it as a source of strength. She realises that in Mme Beck's machinations to keep her and Paul apart, Mme Beck is playing upon Lucy's 'total default of self-assertion' (541). With mounting feeling, however, Lucy is liberated from her 'moral paralysis' (541). In her own terms her diatribe with Mme Beck 'broke out' and Lucy finds she has 'left behind [her] wonted respects and fears' (453). In abandoning acquiescence, Lucy has ceased to collaborate with her own imprisonment. Thus she escapes from the pensionnat on the night of the fête and feels 'wonder at the strange ease with which this prison has been forced' (548).

Lucy's growing perception of herself as an agent rather than a victim is crucial for her development. It allows her to refuse the roles that others would assign to her. So, she rejects the offer to become Paulina's paid companion, tacitly refusing the self-effacement which the role would involve: 'I am no bright lady's shadow' (382). With an 'inward courage' she resists Graham's insensitive coercion when he seeks to enlist Lucy to act as his pander with Paulina. It is an important moment for her self-respect and for her liberation from Graham because she realises with 'now welcome force' that Graham 'wanted always to give me a rôle not mine' (404). With her increasing acceptance of self, Lucy can break free from the thrall of external arbiters of behaviour: 'Whatever my powers – feminine or the contrary – God had given them, and I felt resolute to be ashamed of no faculty of His bestowal' (440). Lucy no longer needs to live her life vicariously through others and rejects her former role as voyeur when she declines Paulina's offer to share her 'beautiful life' with Graham: 'I shall share no man's or woman's life in this world, as you understand sharing. I think I have one friend of my own, but am not sure; and till I *am* sure, I live solitary' (520).

After so much negative feedback, Paul's interest, then jealousy, give Lucy her first sense of sexual power. As she acknowledges after Paul's agitated discourse on her manner of dress, Lucy is 'well habituated to be passed by as a shadow in Life's sunshine: it is a new thing to see one testily lifting his hand to screen his eyes, because you tease him with an obtrusive ray' (421). Lucy's earlier trauma when Mrs Bretton buys her a pink dress stems from her acute uneasiness at any recognition of her sexual identity. She is accordingly most anxious that she not be regarded as 'decking [her]self out to draw attention' (284). It is significant, then, that by the time of the school picnic Lucy wears another pink dress, one of her own choosing this time and worn with a full sense of the impression it will make on Paul. And in keeping with the sexual confidence indicated by Lucy's dress her behaviour with Paul becomes increasingly playful and assertive: 'I listened to him, and did not trouble myself to be too submissive' (452).

Lucy's victories over repression are necessarily accompanied by her developing expression which provides a means of release. In her struggle to keep her feeling for Graham hidden her 'mutinous' self protests, 'But if I feel, may I *never* express?' only to be told '*Never*!' by relentless Reason. That stricture becomes intolerable, however, and Lucy's impulse to find release in expression is given outlet in her visit to the confessional. Nevertheless, that gesture only allows a ritual release, one outside her normal sphere and never to be repeated, and not any more meaningful and decisive action that might impact upon her life. Her outburst against Mme Beck provides a taste of liberation and Lucy finally finds full release in her last encounter with Paul: 'I spoke. All leaped from my lips. I lacked not words now; fast I narrated; fluent I told my tale; it streamed on my tongue' (591).

Given the decisive role that Paul plays in Lucy's development, we might well question why the hero should be banished in the end. The simplest answer is that in this most uncompromising novel Brontë refuses to take refuge in the conventional happy ending. She has prepared the way throughout the novel for Lucy's solitary life at the end. The threat for Caroline in *Shirley* is to be the reality for Lucy in *Villette*. In the opening chapters Miss Marchmont's life story provides a prophetic parallel to Lucy's life and also provides the model of a life lived singly yet enriched for having known love. Lucy feels it is her destiny 'to conduct [life] single-handed' (381), echoing Brontë's own sense 'that I am a *single* woman and likely to be lonely. But it cannot be helped and therefore *imperatively must be borne*' (*LL* IV 6). Lucy must learn the difference between the weakness of excusing oneself from action by maintaining a defeatist sense of life as hopelessly determined and the strength of a stoical acceptance of the disparity between fates and a willingness to 'go forward' regardless. To embrace the former or avoid the latter is to live in bad faith:

It is right to look our life-accounts bravely in the face now and then, and settle them honestly. And he is a poor self-swindler who lies to himself while he reckons the items, and sets down under the head happiness that which is misery. Call anguish – anguish, and despair – despair;

write both down in strong characters with resolute pen: you will the better pay your debt to Doom. Falsify; insert 'privilege' where you should have written 'pain;' and see if your mighty creditor will allow the fraud to pass, or accept the coin with which you would cheat him. Offer to the strongest – if the darkest angel of God's host – water, when he asked blood – will he take it? Not a whole pale sea for one red drop. I settled another account. (451)

By these standards Brontë, too, has 'settled . . . account[s]'.

In considering the novel's ending it is also necessary to realise that life with Paul cannot be seen simply as the ideal fate for Lucy. For all his positive influence on Lucy, there are negative aspects to the relationship. Just as he is liberating, he is, too, repressive. At times, admittedly, his strictures are calculated to provoke opposition – 'to draw from me contradiction or objection' (443) – but at others his behaviour is much less controlled and more disturbing. He conducts a 'constant crusade against the "amour-propre" of every human-being, but himself' (225). Hence his insistence that Lucy not view the portrait of Cleopatra and contemplate instead the conventional 'La vie d'une femme', and his ruthless censorship of the books he lends Lucy and of the stories he reads the class.

Paul is a fiercely competitive man, adverse to self-assured competence in others, and especially in women, as his shameful vendetta against Madame Panache demonstrates: 'He would have exiled fifty Madame de Staels, if they had annoyed, offended, out-rivalled, or opposed him' (436). His competitiveness is evident, too, in his obsessive fear that Lucy knows more than she shows which leads him to set traps to expose her suspected knowledge of Greek and Latin. When Lucy protests that she harbours only 'a knowledge of my own' (444), he is uncomprehending. His desire to see her take the platform on the public examination day is only partially benevolent: 'He wanted to see me worsted (I knew he did)' (446).

Paul enthusiastically participates in Mme Beck's repressive system of 'espionage', regularly rifling Lucy's desk and maintaining a secret watch from his hired rooms. His bullying and sometimes violent temperament aligns him in some respects with the threatening aspects of Lucy's world which underscore her female vulnerability. He locks her into the attic where she shrinks from the sexually suggestive threat of 'the beetles . . . fading from my sight; I trembled lest they should steal on me a march, mount my throne unseen, and unsuspected, invade my skirts' (205). He deprives her of food in her imprisonment as he does again when he keeps her in the oppressive heat of the first classe. He ignores her cry that she wants 'to be liberated, to get out into the air' (446) and reduces her to his 'half-worried prey'. Throughout the novel Paul's dealings with Lucy are frequently imaged in terms of violation, often sexual, as when he bursts 'firm, fast, straight' into the first classe, her 'sanctuary', and his eyes 'hungrily dived into' her (201), or when Paul describes Lucy's response to him as reminiscent of 'a young she wild creature, new caught, untamed, viewing with a mixture of fire and fear the first entrance of the breaker-in' (311).[3]

In the end the school that Paul prepares for Lucy is indicative of his role in her life. From the 'nobody' with 'no home' Lucy has come with Paul's aid to the point where she can identify herself, as the 'fair characters' of the prospectus testify, as 'Mademoiselle Lucy Snowe' of 'Numéro 7, Faubourg Clotilde' (586). It is perhaps significant, though, that the world that Paul prepares for Lucy is fastidiously 'neat' and 'small' in every detail. It is in a sense *his* version of a suitable world for Lucy. Although it delights her, it is revealing that in his absence she expands it. Paul's consideration and generosity have provided Lucy with the opportunity and the challenge to assume real power and to shape her own life. The point of the ending is not that she fails to marry Paul (his death is appropriately uncertain) but that she takes up that challenge.

Despite Lucy's designation of herself as Paul's 'steward', her successes are very much her own. The original plan for the school is Lucy's and the first year's rent comes from Lucy's savings. Through her own hard work and success and with the legacy from Miss Marchmont Lucy expands the school and even reverses roles by creating a space for Paul: 'I have made him a little library' (595). In his absence Lucy spends 'the three happiest years of [her] life' (593), faces the fear of loneliness which has for so long gnawed at her life and discovers it 'a vain thing' (593).

The final lines of the novel are a calm refusal of pity and they represent the culmination of what is perhaps Lucy's principal achievement – the narrative itself. In a carefully and consciously crafted story Lucy has progressed from the deceptions of the beginning to the authority and self-awareness of the ending. She has provided clarification of her own distortions, thereby signalling both her health and her achievement.

7 Critics on Charlotte Brontë

> One thing, however, I see plainly enough, and that is Mr.
> Currer Bell needs improvement, and ought to strive after
> it; and this (D.V.) he honestly intends to do – taking his
> time, however, and following as his guides Nature and
> Truth. If these lead to what the critics call art, it is all very
> well; but if not, that grand desideratum has no chance of
> being run after or caught. (*LL* III 83)

Charlotte Brontë did not suffer from critical neglect in her
lifetime: her genius was never overlooked in the ways that her
sister Emily's was. From the beginning with the sensational
appearance of *Jane Eyre* in October 1847 Charlotte's talent
was almost universally acclaimed. Contemporary critics
repeatedly described her work as 'original' and 'remarkable',
demonstrating 'power', 'vigour', 'truth', 'force' and 'reality'.

Her first published novel was hailed by the distinguished
critic G. H. Lewes as '[d]ecidedly the best novel of the
season' and the *Atlas* declared *Jane Eyre* to be 'not merely a
work of great promise; it is one of absolute performance'.[1]
The critical reception of *Shirley* was generally more moderate, betraying some signs of disappointment at the eagerly
awaited second novel of a controversial author, which was to
confirm or dash the reputation gained by *Jane Eyre*. Brontë
herself deemed the majority of reviews as 'on the whole . . .
favourable' (*LL* III 35), although a harsh review of *Shirley* in
The Times and Lewes's notice in the *Edinburgh Review*
caused her considerable pain. *Villette* stimulated two further

reviews which stung Brontë deeply – one by Harriet
Martineau in the *Daily News* and the other by Anne Mozley
in the *Christian Remembrancer* – but more broadly Charlotte's
last novel was received as 'confirmation of Currer Bell's
genius' (*CH* 178).

Extravagant comparisons and claims for Brontë's status as
a novelist accompanied the notice of her work. The *Era*, for
example, declared in November 1847 that 'all serious novel
writers of the day lose in comparison with Currer Bell'
(*CH* 79) and after the appearance of *Villette* G. H. Lewes
declared in the *Leader*: 'In Passion and Power – those noble
twins of Genius – Currer Bell has no living rival except
George Sand' (*CH* 184).

Even Brontë's detractors, who were heard in increasing
numbers after the initial flush of success with *Jane Eyre*,
acknowledged the power and influence of her work. So, *The
Times*'s savage review of *Shirley* emphasised the second
novel's failure by contrasting it with the first novel's success:
'Millions understood her before – she may count by units
those who will appreciate her now' (*CH* 151). And even
Elizabeth Rigby's infamously vitriolic notice in the *Quarterly
Review* acknowledged, albeit with concern, 'the popularity
of *Jane Eyre*' and remarked upon the combination of
'genuine power with such horrid taste', enabling the *Quarterly*
to claim later with some justice: 'while we felt it may be our
duty to impugn its tendency, we unhesitatingly admitted its
talent' (*CH* 106 and 156).

The success of Charlotte Brontë's novels in her time
testifies to the fact that she struck a chord in the Victorian
reading public. She provided images of rebellion, liberation,
self-respect and power and an acknowledgement of passion
and intuition which captured the imagination of many. At the
same time, though, what was seen by some as inspirational
was seen equally by others as threatening. Her novels were
a challenge to the status quo and as such, for all their acclaim,
they elicited not simply negative critical judgement but

strident condemnation. In order to understand the strength of that reaction it is necessary to appreciate that fiction in the mid-nineteenth century was increasingly seen as a potent form of social commentary which had a direct and potentially formative effect on life. Hence literary reviews made repeated connections between novels and public morality and in 1861 the novelist Dinah Mulock (Mrs Craik) described the contemporary novel as 'one of the most important moral agents of the community. The essayist may write for his hundreds, the preacher preach for his thousands; but the novelist counts his audience by millions. His power is three-fold – over heart, reason and fancy'.[2]

Brontë's novels were seen in some quarters as an offence against the good taste, proper reticence and moral tone of the times. Even enthusiastic reviews frequently regretted the 'coarseness' and 'indelicacy' of Brontë's language and style. The first to do so on 6 November 1847 was the *Spectator*. It referred to the relationship between Jane and Rochester as 'a course of hardly "proper" conduct between a single man and a maiden in her teens' and diagnosed 'a low tone of behaviour in the novel' (*CH* 75). Brontë saw the review, somewhat prematurely, as a sign of things to come: 'I shall expect it to be followed by other notices of a similar nature. The way to detraction has been pointed out, and will probably be pursued' (*LL* II 155).

In fact there was a marked increase in the negative criticism of Charlotte Brontë's work but it did not really emerge for another year. During that time Anne Brontë's second novel *The Tenant of Wildfell Hall* appeared and its scenes of debauchery and domestic violence aroused a degree of moral outrage which may have coloured the perception of the propriety of the other 'Bells', especially since Anne's publisher Newby was systematically attempting to confuse and merge the identity of the three 'brothers' in order to exploit the success of *Jane Eyre*. Then in December 1848 Elizabeth Rigby's resounding attack on *Jane Eyre* appeared in the *Quarterly*. Rigby branded the novel as 'pre-eminently an anti-Christian composition' (*CH* 109), a book 'stamped by a coarseness of language and a laxity of tone' (*CH* 106) and declared that if it was written by a woman, 'we have no alternative but to ascribe it to one who has, for some sufficient reason, long forfeited the society of her own sex' (*CH* 111). Rigby's tone of high moral condemnation made a considerable impact on the climate of opinion, as Brontë herself discovered when she found her novel referred to by a friend as 'a wicked book': 'It opened my eyes to the harm the "Quarterly" had done' (*LL* III 23).

A third factor contributing to the change in tone in the critical discussion of Brontë's work was the growing speculation, confirmed as certainty by the time *Shirley* appeared in October 1849, that Currer Bell was a woman. From the first critics seemed to feel compelled to ascertain the sex of the author of *Jane Eyre* and the energy that went into the debate on the matter rivalled any more genuinely critical concern in the reviews. The crudity of the criteria for assessing the author's gender is evident from a comparison of the reviews. *Era*, for example, declared: 'It is no woman's writing . . . no woman *could have* penned the "Autobiography of Jane Eyre"' (*CH* 79), while G. H. Lewes observed with confidence in *Fraser's Magazine* that the 'writer is evidently a woman' (*CH* 84). The *North American Review* resolved the enigma by adopting an improbable middle line: 'The work bears marks of more than one mind and one sex' (*CH* 98).

This preoccupation with the gender of the author reflected not simply idle curiosity but a desire to categorise writer and text within a conventional framework. Critical opinion was shaped by a prescriptive set of assumptions about what was expected of women writers and what they were capable of. The consequent double standard lay behind G. H. Lewes's warning to Brontë that she must not suffer her style 'to wander into such vulgarities as would be inexcusable – even in a man' (*CH* 165), and repeatedly reviewers found ele-

ments of Brontë's work unacceptable from the pen of a
woman. Her presentation of sexual passion was seen as
particularly offensive – her characters 'unfeminine' in their
display of emotion, and her feelings 'vehement and deep, but
stern and masculine in their character and modes of expression' (*CH* 193).

In review after review sexist assumptions masqueraded as
literary judgements:

> . . . literary stereotypes adapted very slowly to any real
> evidence of feminine achievement. If we break down the
> categories that are the staple of Victorian periodical
> reviewing, we find that women writers were acknowledged
> to possess sentiment, refinement, tact, observation,
> domestic expertise, high moral tone, and knowledge of
> female character; and thought to lack originality, intellec-
> tual training, abstract intelligence, humor, self-control,
> and knowledge of male character. Male writers had most of
> the desirable qualities: power, breadth, distinctness, clar-
> ity, learning, abstract intelligence, shrewdness, experi-
> ence, humor, knowledge of everyone's character, and
> open-mindedness.[3]

In such a scheme female authors were inevitably disadvantaged. So, when the *Christian Remembrancer* declared of *Jane
Eyre* that it would be hard to find a book in the annals of
female authorship 'more unfeminine both in its excellences
and defects' (*CH* 89), Charlotte Brontë was damned both
ways – in her defects she failed her sex and in her excellences she transcended it. Even G. H. Lewes, who was in
many ways genuinely receptive to the real power of
Brontë's book, betrayed signs of the prevailing sexism in his
reviews. He wrote of *Jane Eyre*, for example, as a 'masculine
book in the sense of vigour' and regretted the same 'over-
masculine vigour' in *Shirley*. When he declared in his *Jane*

Eyre review that 'unless a novel be built out of real experience, it can have no real success', he discounted the power of the imagination in a way particularly damaging for women, whose experience might be expected to be more limited within the social arrangements of the day. And in his review of *Shirley*, which made Brontë 'wish in future he would leave me alone, and not write what makes me feel so cold and sick' (*LL* III 66), Lewes took the opportunity to speculate on the limited achievements of female artists and dogmatise: 'The grand function of woman, it must always be recollected, is, and ever must be, Maternity' (*CH* 161).

It is easier to understand the arrogance of Lewes's position, if we recognise that underlying the general discussion of women's literature lay a concern for woman's place and behind the hostility that Brontë's novels inspired was frequently a fear of a rebellious threat to the status quo. This is clear in the terminology used in the *Christian Remembrancer*'s attack on *Jane Eyre*. 'Every page', it contended, 'burns with moral Jacobinism' (*CH* 90). The *Quarterly* saw Jane Eyre as the 'personification of an unregenerate and undisciplined spirit' and her sin, though termed 'pride' was equally self-reliance: 'It is by her own talents, virtues, and courage that she is made to attain the summit of human happiness' (*CH* 109). Its condemnation culminated in the most explicit identification of the novel as a political and social threat:

. . . there is that pervading tone of ungodly discontent which is at once the most prominent and the most subtle evil which the law and the pulpit, which all civilized society in fact has at the present day to contend with. We do not hesitate to say that the tone of the mind and thought which has overthrown authority and violated every code human and divine abroad, and fostered Chartism and rebellion at home, is the same which has also written Jane Eyre. (*CH* 110)

The *Athenaeum* subsequently went further in November 1849 and linked *Shirley* not merely to a general social unrest but specifically to movements for the liberation of women. It claimed that the novel's heroines 'both suffer from the malady of unrest and dissatisfaction, – on the prevalence of which among women of the nineteenth century so many protests have been issued, so many theories of "emancipation" have been set forth' (*CH* 123).

The French critic, Eugène Forçade, offered a revealing perspective upon the English response in his notice of *Shirley* in the *Revue des deux mondes*. He saw *Shirley* as a book about the '*condition of women*' which defended the cause of women with 'a conviction and a skill perfectly characteristic of those who are pleading their own cause' (*CH* 143). While himself valuing 'the moral freedom, the spirit of insubordination [and] the impulses of revolt against certain social conventions' he found in both *Jane Eyre* and *Shirley*, Forçade could astutely characterise the social tensions underlying Brontë's critical reception in England:

> *Jane Eyre* bore the accent of revolt against certain social conventions and contained aspirations to independence which frightened conservative critics who saw them as a threat. . . . Those writers who stand guard over the traditional values of English society were harsh in their denunciation of these tendencies. *Jane Eyre* was reproached with having been intended as an attack on marriage and the social order. (*CH* 143)

Charlotte Brontë was by no means immune to the critical attacks on her work. In a letter to W. S. Williams, for example, she acknowledged that she was 'distressed' to find that the *Spectator* 'seemed to have found more harm than good in "Jane Eyre"' (*LL* II 155). After Emily's and Anne's deaths, feeling 'that almost all supports have been withdrawn', Charlotte was more vulnerable to the judgement of critics: 'Were my sisters now alive they and I would laugh over this notice; but they sleep, they will wake no more for me, and I am a fool to be so moved by what is not worth a sigh' (*LL* III 30). She was understandably most hurt by the negative criticism of those she respected. So, with the reviews of both G. H. Lewes and Harriet Martineau she felt a mixture of personal and professional betrayal.

Importantly, however, Charlotte was unbowed by the attacks and passionately committed to her own sense of artistic truth. She offered a rejoinder to Elizabeth Rigby's attack in her 'Word to the "Quarterly"' which she intended to serve as a Preface for *Shirley*. She was oppressed by the critics' hunt for the gender of Currer Bell, asking her publisher with exasperation: 'Why can they not be content to take Currer Bell for a man?' (*LL* III 34), and when she felt that Lewes had revealed his own sexist double standards, she did not hesitate to confront him:

> I will tell you why I was so hurt by that review in the 'Edinburgh' – not because its criticism was keen or its blame sometimes severe; not because its praise was stinted (for, indeed, I think you give me quite as much praise as I deserve), but because after I had said earnestly that I wished critics would judge me as an *author*, not as a woman, you so roughly – I even thought so cruelly – handled the question of sex. I dare say you meant no harm and perhaps you will not now be able to understand why I was so grieved at what you will probably deem such a trifle; but grieved I was, and indignant too.
>
> There was a passage or two which you did quite wrong to write. (*LL* III 68)

In all, with a truth to self worthy of her heroines, Charlotte Brontë declared: 'I am ashamed of nothing I have written – not a line' (*LL* III 25).

Following her death in March 1855 a series of tributes

appeared. Harriet Martineau, Elizabeth Gaskell and William Thackeray in turn praised the woman as much as the work, making claims for her strength, courage, integrity and 'impetuous honesty'. Gaskell, in particular, in her desire to create 'a right understanding of the life of my dear friend' assumed a tone of impassioned advocacy: 'Think of her home . . . think of her father's sight hanging on a thread . . . and then admire as it deserves to be admired, the steady courage which could work away at *Jane Eyre*'.[4] The details of Brontë's life allayed further speculation about the morality of Currer Bell as a woman who must have 'long forfeited the society of her own sex'. Reviewers were noticeably more well-disposed towards Brontë and the tone of harsh moralism softened: 'But as we recall the lone woman sitting by the desolate hearthstone, and remember all that she lost and suffered, we cannot blame very gravely the occasional harshness and impatience of her language when dealing with men who have been cast in a different mould' (*CH* 341). It is worth noting, though, that if the result of the eulogy following her death was less negative judgement, the basis for the judgement remained largely the same – the artist came second to the woman, the art was answerable to the life.

Nevertheless, Charlotte Brontë was certainly more highly acclaimed and in some respects more justly dealt with in her own time than in subsequent decades. By 1877 when T. W. Reid's biography *Charlotte Brontë, A Monograph* appeared Reid was expressing regret at the 'recent' neglect of the Brontë novels: 'though fresh editions have recently been issued they have had no circulation worthy of being compared with that which they maintained between 1850 and 1860' (*CH* 398). Similarly, Swinburne characterised his extravagant claims for the 'genius of Charlotte Brontë' as 'unfashionable' in 1877 in his *Charlotte Brontë. A Note*.

Leslie Stephen's reply to Swinburne's *Note* in *Cornhill* in December 1877 proved a landmark in establishing criteria

for the judgement of Charlotte Brontë's work, the influence
of which can be traced right through to Lord David Cecil's
important essays on Charlotte and Emily in *Early Victorian
Novelists* in 1934 and in some measure to the New Criticism
of the 1940's. Stephen's requirements of the critic – the need
to establish a 'scientific basis' for criticism resting upon
'purely rational ground' – can be seen as a reaction against
Swinburne's florrid prose but also signal values and assumptions which would inevitably blind him to some of the
strengths of Brontë's fiction. Stephen admires her penetrat-
ing 'powers of observation', for example, but sees them as
'restricted by circumstances and narrowed by the limitations
of her intellect'. He laments her 'want of comprehensiveness'
and her 'deadly' earnestness. He sees her 'admirable flashes
of vivid expression' as liable to give way to a 'strangely
contorted' prose because of the 'feverish disquiet' of her
novels. The mind that created *Villette* is in his view 'radically
inconsistent and tentative'. A more powerful intellect would
'even under her conditions have worked out some more
comprehensible and harmonious solution'. Stephen, in con-
tending that 'the study of her life is the study of her novels'
and her characters are 'more or less mouthpieces', discounts
the creative power of Brontë's work, while enshrining the
subjective as a lesser art. In many ways it is an astute essay
which has no time for the earlier moralism of the 'luckless
critics who blundered so hopelessly' and failed to recognise
the 'instinctive nobility' of Brontë's spirit. However in
setting up ideals of objectivity, decisiveness and unity it
provided a set of criteria against which Brontë's novels were
assessed as lacking for a long time to come (*CH* 413–23).

At the turn of the century, for example, Mary Ward's
wide-ranging introductions to the Haworth edition of the
Brontës' work show signs of Stephen's influence. While
claiming a place for Charlotte Brontë with the 'immortals',
Ward accepts Stephen's judgement about Brontë's narrow-

ness. She sees 'personality' as the 'sole but sufficient spell' of Brontë's novels, is still preoccupied in some measure with Charlotte's bad taste – her 'lack of social intelligence' – and discounts the radical force of Brontë's work: 'No judgment was ever more foolish that that which detected a social rebel in the writer of *Jane Eyre*' (*CH* 453).

Where Ward differs from Stephen, and reflects a growing trend of the 1880's, is in her estimation of Emily as the greater of the two sisters: 'The difference between them is almost wholly in Emily's favour'. Ironically, though, the basic grounds for her judgement recall Stephen's critical criteria. Ward contends that Emily's work is not flawed by the subjectivity of Charlotte's: where Emily remains 'hidden and self-contained' as an artist, Charlotte is intrusive and betrays a 'lack of literary reticence'.

Lord David Cecil decisively confirmed Charlotte's secondary position to Emily with his essays on the two sisters in *Early Victorian Novelists* in 1934. More importantly, although purporting to describe Charlotte Brontë as a 'genius' who could not be 'dismissed to a minor rank', Cecil's reservations were infinitely more damning than his praise and thirty years later Mildred Christian still described Cecil's essay as having dealt a blow to Charlotte Brontë's reputation as an artist 'from which it has never fully recovered'.[5]

Cecil's essay stresses Brontë's failure as a 'craftsman': she has 'no gift of form, no restraint, little power of observation, no power of analysis'. In Cecil's discussion apparent merits quickly take on the aspect of faults. Thus, he accords Brontë the status of being the 'first subjective novelist', anticipating Proust and Joyce, but then declares that unlike her male descendants Brontë lacks the detachment to analyse her subjective material: her novels 'are not exercises of the mind, but cries of the heart'; not a deliberate self-diagnosis, but an involuntary self-revelation. Once again the complexity of Brontë's art is denied. Brontë is seen as 'naive' and 'crude' and her achievement is equated with her personality: 'And a very odd one it is', marked by 'extreme simplicity' and 'alarming innocence'.

Cecil contends that Brontë's failure of craft is redeemed by her creative imagination. However, once more that saving grace becomes a limitation as 'unhelped as she is by any great power of observation and analysis, her world is almost exclusively an imaginary world'. Brontë's style is 'turbid and irregular' lacking the 'exact translucency of the true stylist'. Finally, recalling Stephen's criticism but revealing a tone more patronising and reductive, Cecil declares: 'Once fully launched on her surging flood of self-revelation, Charlotte Brontë is far above pausing to attend to so paltry a consideration as artistic unity'.[6]

Virginia Woolf's was the voice that might have stood out against the tide for Charlotte Brontë, as she had for other women writers both in particular and in general. In 1916 Woolf responded to Brontë's rebellious 'ferocity' and saw it as a source of power, but by 1928 in *A Room of One's Own* Woolf had come to value an androgynous ideal which saw it as 'fatal for a woman to lay stress on any grievance; to plead even with justice any cause; in any way to speak consciously as a woman'.[7] In this light Woolf saw anger as 'tampering with the integrity of Charlotte Brontë the novelist . . . we constantly feel an acidity which is the result of oppression, a buried suffering smouldering beneath her passion, a rancour which contracts those books, splendid as they are, with a spasm of pain'. Therein sounds the echo of Woolf's father, Leslie Stephen, 50 years before, regretting the 'mind diseased' which could not work out 'some more comprehensible and harmonious solution'.

With the emergence of New Criticism in the 1940's and 50's the discussion of Brontë avoided at least the conflation of author and character, biography and fiction. However so long as the author was severed from the text, the historical and sociological relevance of Brontë's work tended to be lost as well. In any case New Criticism's concentration on text and form with preeminence accorded to internal coherence, integration and unity (recalling Stephen's valuing of harmony) ensured that the reputation of Brontë's novels remained comparatively eclipsed.

In 1948 F. R. Leavis proposed his Great Tradition of English novelists. Given Leavis's affinity with many 'new critical' standards, including a valuation of 'formal unity', it is hardly surprising to find Charlotte Brontë excluded from that 'tradition'. However it is revealing to measure Brontë against Leavis's criteria for a great novelist. He contends that a novelist is major 'in the sense that they not only change the possibilities of art for practitioners and readers, but that they are significant in terms of that human awareness they promote; awareness of the possibilities of life'.[8] By those standards one might reasonably expect Charlotte Brontë to be included in such a canon and her exclusion leads one to question how relevant the gender of the critic is in the judgements made. Is 'human' a truly generic and neutral term as it appears? Exactly whose 'tradition' is being constructed? Leavis does not engage at all with the talent of the Brontës. Instead he dismisses Charlotte: 'It is tempting to retort there is only one Brontë. Actually, Charlotte, though claiming no part in the great line of English fiction . . . has a permanent interest of a minor kind'. Emily fares a little better. She is seen as a 'genius, of course' but *Wuthering Heights*, though 'astonishing', seems to Leavis 'a kind of sport'.[9]

In 1960 D. W. Crompton could appeal to a critical consensus on the comparatively minor significance of Charlotte Brontë's novels: 'one is still left with the fact (which cannot be argued here but is at least generally accepted) that *Wuthering Heights* is a great book and that *Jane Eyre* – whatever its structure – is relatively miniature in conception and execution and yields little more from sustained consideration than it does from a single reading'.[10] The last 25 years, however, have seen a marked rehabilitation in Charlotte Brontë's reputation principally through the agency of two distinct schools of criticism.

The first development has explicitly challenged views like Crompton's by a close and sustained textual focus on Brontë's novels. Showing signs of the influence of New Criticism, this mode of criticism has eschewed questions of biography and sought to establish the artistry of Charlotte Brontë's work: 'to show that she is more than the inspired improviser and fictionalised autobiographer that she was long considered to be'.[11] Full-length studies in this vein include Robert Martin's *The Accents of Persuasion: Charlotte Brontë's Novels* (1966), Wendy Craik's *The Brontë Novels* (1968), Earl A. Knies's *The Art of Charlotte Brontë* (1969), Karl Kroeber's *Styles in Fictional Structure: The Art of Jane Austen, Charlotte Brontë and George Eliot* (1971) and Margot Peters's *Charlotte Brontë: Style in the Novel* (1973).

The second development which has had an even more decisive effect on the critical perception of Charlotte Brontë has been the emergence of feminist criticism. In many ways feminism has reoriented the whole discussion of literature by women, instituting a new politics 'of *asking women's questions*' and stimulating a radical revaluation of the critical givens of a predominantly male literary establishment.[12]

Feminist 're-vision' has taken place on a number of fronts. The importance of interdisciplinary study for an understanding of the socio-historical context in which the Brontës produced their novels is evident in Inga-Stina Ewbank's *Their Proper Sphere: a Study of the Brontë Sisters as Early Victorian Novelists* (1966), which saw the Brontës' work as part of a continuing tradition of women's literature, and Harriet Bjork's *The Language of Truth: Charlotte Brontë, the Woman Question, and the Novel* (1974), which assessed Brontë's response to contemporary social thought.[13] More generally, pioneering work which inevitably touched upon Charlotte Brontë has been done by critics such as Ellen

Moers in *Literary Women* (1976) and Elaine Showalter in *A Literature of Their Own* (1977) – and before them Patricia Thomson in *The Victorian Heroine: A Changing Ideal, 1837–1873* (1956) – in an effort to chart a female literary tradition: 'to construct a more reliable map from which to explore the achievements of English women novelists'.[14]

Feminist critics have also asserted the value and importance both for reader and writer of issues and concerns specifically relating to women and women's experience. In 1968 Hazel Martin's *Petticoat Rebels: A Study of the Novels of Social Protest by George Eliot, Elizabeth Gaskell, and Charlotte Brontë* appeared and a year later Kate Millet again took up the issue of Charlotte Brontë's writing as rebellion in *Sexual Politics*. A host of books and articles since then have demonstrated the capacity of feminism to invest the critic with 'fresh eyes' with which to 'enter an old text from a new critical direction' as, for example, with Adrienne Rich's important essay in *Ms.* magazine in 1973, '*Jane Eyre*: The Temptations of a Motherless Woman'.

Feminist theory has also contributed to a more complex and controversial sense of the qualities of women's writing. On the one hand critics like Mary Ellmann in *Thinking About Women* (1968) have challenged stereotypes of feminine formlessness, irrationality, spirituality and the like. On the other some feminist critics, particularly influenced by trends in French criticism, have sought to explore the distinctive femaleness of prose by women and give to 'the idea of *difference* a new and positive force'.[15] The result has been a stimulating controversy over female aesthetics, and the efforts of some critics such as Sandra Gilbert and Susan Gubar in *The Madwoman in the Attic: The Woman Writer and the Nineteenth-Century Imagination* (1979) to analyse the qualities of the female imagination. Accordingly, qualities such as objectivity, unity and rationality are no longer accepted as the *sine qua non* of literary merit and importance. When Matthew Arnold wrote in 1853 that Charlotte Brontë's mind contained 'nothing but hunger, rebellion and rage' the condemnation was self-evident. Feminists today might rather take the comment as a starting point for an examination of the way in which anger and rebelliousness vitalised the work of Charlotte Brontë and inspired the women who read her.

Notes

Notes to Chapter 1

1. Quoted in Elaine Showalter, *A Literature of Their Own: British Women Novelists from Brontë to Lessing* (London, Virago, 1982), p. 106.
2. *The Brontës: Their Lives, Friendships and Correspondence*, eds T. J. Wise and J. A. Symington (Oxford, Shakespeare Head, 1934), II, p. 338. All further references appear in the text abbreviated as *LL*.
3. Maria Brontë is reported to have died of cancer. However gynaecologists have since speculated that she died of a disorder which stemmed from her rapid childbearing. See Phillip Rhodes, 'A Medical Appraisal of the Brontës', *Brontë Society Transactions*, 16, 2 (1971).
4. Quoted in Margot Peters *Unquiet Soul: a Biography of Charlotte Brontë* (London, Hodder and Stoughton, 1975), p. 9.
5. Quoted in Tillie Olsen, *Silences* (New York, Delta, 1973), p. 233.
6. Fanny Ratchford and William de Vane (eds), *Legends of Angria* (New Haven, Yale University Press, 1933), p. 316.
7. Quoted in Elizabeth Gaskell *The Life of Charlotte Brontë* (London, Dent, 1971), p. 399.
8. 'A Medical Appraisal of the Brontës', op. cit., pp. 101–9.
9. John Maynard, *Charlotte Brontë and Sexuality* (Cambridge, Cambridge University Press, 1984), pp. 218–24. Dr. Weiss also questions Rhodes's definition of *hyperemesis gravidarum* as a psychosomatic illness.
10. William Blackstone's *Commentaries on the English Constitution* (1758) outlined the 'civil death' women underwent in marriage. For a detailed discussion of the marriage laws see John Stuart Mill *The Subjection of Women* (London, Dent, 1982), Ch. 2.
11. John Stuart Mill, ibid., p. 247.
12. Elizabeth Gaskell, op. cit., p. 238.
13. Florence Nightingale 'Cassandra', Appendix 1, Ray Strachey *The Cause: a Short History of the Women's Movement in Great Britain* (London, Bell, 1928), p. 396.
14. John Stuart Mill, op. cit., p. 259.

Notes to Chapter 2

1. Quoted in Sandra Gilbert and Susan Gubar, *The Madwoman in the Attic: The Woman Writer and the Nineteenth-Century Literary Imagination* (New Haven, Yale University Press, 1979), p. 539.
2. Kathleen Tillotson, *Novels of the Eighteen-Forties* (Oxford, Oxford University Press, 1956), p. 149.

3. Robert Heilman, 'Charlotte Brontë's "New" Gothic' in *The Victorian Novel: Modern Essays in Criticism*, ed. Ian Watt (New York, Oxford University Press, 1971), pp. 165–80.

4. Quoted in Elaine Showalter, op. cit., p. 106.

5. Terry Eagleton, *Myths of Power: A Marxist Study of the Brontës* (London, Macmillan, 1975), p. 76.

6. George Saintsbury, 'The Position of the Brontës as Origins in the History of the English Novel', *Brontë Society Transactions*, II (April 1899), p. 25.

7. S. Gilbert and S. Gubar, op. cit., p. xi.

8. See Ch. 6, pp. 86–8.

9. Margot Peters interprets these devices as 'a negative delight in going against the grain'. *Charlotte Brontë: Style in the Novel* (Madison, University of Wisconsin Press, 1973), p. 57.

10. See Ch. 6, p. 97.

11. As the Inner London Education Authority did in banning her books from school libraries in 1984.

Notes to Chapter 3

1. Fannie Ratchford and William De Vane (eds), *Legends of Angria* (New Haven, Yale University Press, 1933), p. 316.

2. *The Professor* (London, Dent, 1980), p. xi. All subsequent page references in the chapter refer to this edition.

3. See Chapter 1, p. 8.

4. Helene Moglen, *Charlotte Brontë: the Self Conceived* (New York, Norton, 1976), p. 88.

5. See Chapter 5, p. 78.

Notes to Chapter 4

1. *Jane Eyre*, World Classics edn (Oxford, Oxford University Press, 1980), p. 242. All subsequent page references in the chapter refer to this edition.

Notes to Chapter 5

1. Helene Moglen does so very interestingly, for example, claiming that the novel's theme is 'nothing less than the misuse of power within a patriarchal society'. Op. cit., p. 158.

2. *Shirley*, World Classics edn (Oxford, Oxford University Press, 1981), p. 63.

Notes to Chapter 6

1. *Villette* (Middlesex, Penguin, 1981), p. 564. All subsequent page references in the chapter refer to this edition.
2. Helene Moglen, op. cit., p. 203.
3. For a fuller discussion of this aspect of the novel see Pauline Nestor, *Female Friendships and Communities: Charlotte Brontë, George Eliot, Elizabeth Gaskell* (Oxford, Oxford University Press, 1985), pp. 132–4.

Notes to Chapter 7

1. Miriam Allott (ed.), *The Brontës: The Critical Heritage* (London, Routledge and Kegan Paul, 1974), pp. 87 and 67. *The Critical Heritage* provides an invaluable resource on the critical reception of Brontë's novels and will hereafter be abbreviated in the text as *CH*.
2. Dinah Mulock, 'To Novelists – and a Novelist', *Macmillan's Magazine*, April 1861, p. 442.
3. Elaine Showalter, op. cit., p. 90.
4. Elizabeth Gaskell, op. cit., pp. 6 and 213.
5. Mildred Christian in *Victorian Fiction: A Guide to Research*, ed. Lionel Stevenson (Cambridge, Mass., Harvard University Press, 1964), p. 230.
6. David Cecil, *Early Victorian Novelists: Essays in Revaluation* (London, Constable, 1960), p. 116.
7. Virginia Woolf, *A Room of One's Own* (Middlesex, Penguin, 1974), p. 102. This approach anticipates Carolyn Heilbrun's in 1973 in *Towards the Recognition of Androgyny* (New York, Harper Colophon, 1974).
8. F. R. Leavis, *The Great Tradition* (Middlesex, Penguin, 1967) p. 10.
9. F. R. Leavis, ibid, p. 37.
10. D. W. Crompton, 'The New Criticism: A Caveat', *Essays in Criticism*, 10 (1960), p. 362.
11. Earl A. Knies, *The Art of Charlotte Brontë* (Athens, Ohio University Press, 1969), p. ix.
12. Adrienne Rich, *On Lies, Secrets and Silence: Selected Prose 1960–1978* (New York, Norton, 1979), p. 17.
13. Without a specifically feminist interest, other recent studies have sought to present a contextual understanding of Charlotte Brontë's work. See, for example, Robert Colby, *Fiction with a Purpose* (1967), Tom Winnifrith, *The Brontës and Their Background* (1973) and Terry Eagleton, *Myths of Power: A Marxist Study of the Brontës* (1975).
14. Elaine Showalter, op. cit., p. vii.
15. Ruth Gounelas, 'Charlotte Brontë and the Critics: Attitudes to the Female Qualities in her Writing', *Journal of the Australasian Universities Language and Literature Association*, 62 (Nov. 1984), p. 165.

Bibliography

Selected Works by Charlotte Brontë

The Brontës: Their Lives, Friendships and Correspondence, eds T. J. Wise and J. A. Symington, 4 vols (Oxford, Shakespeare Head, 1932).

Emma a Fragment (1860) in *The Professor and Emma a Fragment* (London, Dent, 1980).

Five Novelettes, ed. Winifred Gérin (London, Folio Press, 1971).

Jane Eyre, World Classics edn (Oxford, Oxford University Press, 1980).

The Miscellanies and Unpublished Writings of Charlotte and Patrick Brontë, eds T. J. Wise and J. A. Symington, 2 vols (Oxford, Shakespeare Head, 1934).

Poems by Acton, Ellis and Currer Bell (London, Aylott and Jones, 1846).

The Professor (London, Dent, 1980).

Shirley, World Classics edn (Oxford, Oxford University Press, 1981).

Tales from Angria, ed. Phyllis Bentley (London, Collins, 1954).

Villette (Middlesex, Penguin, 1981).

Selected Works about Charlotte Brontë

Adams, Maurianne, '*Jane Eyre*: Woman's Estate' in *The Authority of Experience: Essays in Feminist Criticism*, eds A. Diamond and Lee R. Edwards (Amherst, University of Massachusetts Press, 1977), pp. 137–59.

Alexander, Christine, *The Early Writings of Charlotte Brontë* (Oxford, Blackwell, 1983).

Allott, Miriam (ed.), *The Brontës: the Critical Heritage* (London, Routledge and Kegan Paul, 1974).

Basch, Françoise, *Relative Creatures: Victorian Women in Society and the Novel 1837–67*, trans. Anthony Rudolf (London, Allen Lane, 1974).

Beer, Patricia, *Reader, I Married Him: a Study of the Women Characters of Jane Austen, Charlotte Brontë and George Eliot* (London, Macmillan, 1974).

Bjork, Harriet, *The Language of Truth: Charlotte Brontë, the Woman Question, and the Novel* (Lund, Sweden; Gleerup, 1974).

Burkhart, Charles, *Charlotte Brontë: a Psychosexual Study of her Novels* (London, Gollancz, 1973).

Cecil, David, Lord, *Early Victorian Novelists: Essays in Revaluation* (London, Constable, 1960).

Christian, Mildred G., 'The Brontës' in *Victorian Fiction: A Guide to Research*, ed. Lionel Stevenson (Cambridge, Mass.; Harvard University Press, 1964).

Colby, Robert, *Fiction with a Purpose: Major and Minor Nineteenth-Century Novels* (Bloomington, Indiana University Press, 1967).

Colby, Vineta, *The Singular Anomaly: Women Novelists of the Nineteenth Century* (London, University of London Press, 1970).

Craik, Wendy, *The Brontë Novels* (London, Methuen, 1968).

Crompton, Donald, 'The New Criticism: A Caveat', *Essays in Criticism*, 10 (1960), pp. 359–64.

Eagleton, Terry, *Myths of Power: A Marxist Study of the Brontës* (London, Macmillan, 1975).

Ellmann, Mary, *Thinking About Women* (London, Macmillan, 1969).

Ewbank, Inga-Stina, *Their Proper Sphere: a Study of the Brontë Sisters as Early Victorian Female Novelists* (London, Edward Arnold, 1966).

Figes, Eva, *Sex and Subterfuge: Women Novelists to 1850* (London, Macmillan, 1982).

Gaskell, Elizabeth, *The Life of Charlotte Brontë* (London, Dent, 1974).

Gérin, Winifred, *Charlotte Brontë: the Evolution of Genius* (Oxford, Oxford University Press, 1967).

Gilbert, Sandra and Gubar, Susan, *The Madwoman in the Attic: The Woman Writer and the Nineteenth-Century Literary Imagination* (New Haven, Yale University Press, 1979).

Gounelas, Ruth, 'Charlotte Brontë and the Critics: Attitudes to the Female Qualities in her Writing', *Journal of the*

120   BIBLIOGRAPHY

Australasian Universities Language and Literature Association, 62 (Nov. 1984), pp. 151–70.

Heilbrun, Carolyn, *Towards a Recognition of Androgyny* (New York, Harpur Colophon, 1974).

Heilman, Robert, 'Charlotte Brontë's "New" Gothic' in *The Victorian Novel: Modern Essays in Criticism*, ed. Ian Watt (New York, Oxford University Press, 1971), pp. 165–80.

Knies, Earl, *The Art of Charlotte Brontë* (Athens, Ohio University Press, 1969).

Kroeber, Karl, *Styles in Fictional Structure: The Art of Jane Austen, Charlotte Brontë and George Eliot* (Princeton, Princeton University Press, 1971).

Leavis, F. R., *The Great Tradition* (Middlesex, Penguin, 1974).

Leavis, Q. D., Introduction to *Jane Eyre* (Middlesex, Penguin, 1966).

Martin, Hazel, *Petticoat Rebels: A Study of the Novels of Social Protest of George Eliot, Elizabeth Gaskell and Charlotte Brontë* (New York, Helios, 1968).

Martin, Robert, B., *The Accents of Persuasion: Charlotte Brontë's Novels* (London, Macmillan, 1978).

Maynard, John, *Charlotte Brontë and Sexuality* (Cambridge, Cambridge University Press, 1984).

Mill, John Stewart, *The Subjection of Women* (London, Dent, 1982).

Millett, Kate, *Sexual Politics* (New York, Doubleday, 1980).

Moers, Ellen, *Literary Women* (New York, Doubleday, 1976).

Moglen, Helene S., *Charlotte Brontë: the Self Conceived* (New York, Norton, 1976).

Mulock, Dinah, 'To Novelists – and a Novelist', *Macmillan's Magazine*, April 1861, pp. 441–48.

Nestor, Pauline, *Female Friendships and Communities: Charlotte Brontë, George Eliot, Elizabeth Gaskell* (Oxford, Oxford University Press, 1985).

Nightingale, Florence, 'Cassandra', in *The Cause: a Short History of the Women's Movement in Great Britain* by Ray Strachey (London, Bell, 1928).

Ohmann, Carol, 'Historical Realitity and "Divine Appointment" in Charlotte Brontë's Fiction', *Signs: Journal of Women in Culture & Society*, Vol. 2, No. 4 (Summer 1977), pp. 757–58.

Olsen, Tillie, *Silences* (New York, Delta, 1979).

Pell, Nancy, 'Resistance, Rebellion, and Marriage: The Economics of *Jane Eyre*', *Nineteenth Century Fiction*, 31 (March 1977), pp. 397–420.

Peters, Margot, *Charlotte Brontë: Style in the Novel* (Madison, University of Wisconsin Press, 1973).

—— *Unquiet Soul: a Biography of Charlotte Brontë* (London, Hodder and Stoughton, 1975).

Ratchford, F. E., *The Brontës' Web of Childhood* (New York, Columbia University Press, 1941).

Ratchford, F. E. and De Vane, William (eds), *Legends of Angria* (New Haven, Yale University Press, 1933).

Rhodes, Phillip, 'A Medical Appraisal of the Brontës', *Brontë Society Transactions*, 16, 2 (1971), pp. 101–9.

Rich, Adrienne, *On Lies, Secrets and Silences: Selected Prose 1966–1978* (New York, Norton, 1979).

Rigney, Barbara Hill, *Madness and Sexual Politics in the Feminist Novel: Studies in Brontë, Woolf, Lessing and Atwood* (Madison, University of Wisconsin Press, 1978).

Rowe, Karen, '"Fairy-born and Human-bred": Jane Eyre's Education in Romance', *The Voyage In: Fictions of Female Development*, eds Elizabeth Abel et al. (Hanover, University Press of New England, 1983), pp. 69–89.

Saintsbury, George, 'The Position of the Brontës as Origins in the History of the English Novel', *Brontë Society Transactions*, II (April 1899), pp. 18–30.

Showalter, Elaine, *A Literature of Their Own: British Women Novelists from Brontë to Lessing* (London, Virago, 1979).

Spivak, Gayatri Chakravorty, 'Three Women's Texts and a Critique of Imperialism', *Critical Inquiry*, Autumn 1975.

Strachey, Ray, *The Cause: a Short History of the Women's Movement in Great Britain* (London, Bell, 1928).

Thomson, Patricia, *The Victorian Heroine: a Changing Ideal, 1837–1873* (London, Oxford University Press, 1956).

Tillotson, Kathleen, *Novels of the Eighteen-Forties* (Oxford, Oxford University Press, 1956).

Winnifrith, Tom, *The Brontës and Their Background* (London, Macmillan, 1977).

Woolf, Virginia, *A Room of One's Own* (Middlesex, Penguin, 1974).

Index

49